# 100 IDE,
## FOR TEACHING
## RELIGIOUS EDUCATION

## CONTINUUM ONE HUNDREDS SERIES

# 100 IDEAS
# FOR TEACHING
# RELIGIOUS
# EDUCATION

*Cavan Wood*

continuum

**Continuum International Publishing Group**

The Tower Building          80 Maiden Lane
11 York Road                Suite 704
London SE1 7NX              New York NY 10038

www.continuumbooks.com

**British Library Cataloguing-in-Publication Data**
A catalogue record for this book is available from the British
Library.

ISBN: 9781847062307 (paperback)

**Library of Congress Cataloging-in-Publication Data**
A catalog record of this book is available from the Library of
Congress.

Designed and typeset by Ben Cracknell Studios | www.benstudios.co.uk
Printed and bound in Great Britain

# CONTENTS

## SECTION 3 **Outside help**

## SECTION 4 **Starters and plenaries**

## SECTION 5 **Cross-curricular links**

# SECTION 6 **Writing approaches**

# SECTION 7 **The Arts**

# SECTION 10  **A final word**

# INTRODUCTION

When the first National Curriculum document came out in 1988, it had on its front cover a number of squares, self-contained units, each of which represented a different subject. When the revised curriculum was issued in 2007, these squares were replaced by a series of intertwining strands, to show that we should see the connections between subjects and not the divisions. Religious Education lends itself to be delivered in many different ways. Using the techniques that pupils might find in English, Geography, History, Citizenship or even Mathematics is a good way to introduce them to some topics within the subject. Ideas that might be found in Drama or PSHE will help pupils to see that active learning approaches are useful when trying to understand new ideas and stories. As RE is concerned with the spiritual, the use of Art and model-making can encourage the development of the importance of symbolism in order to explain or illustrate truths that might be difficult to put into words.

With the rapid increase of pupils taking full and short courses at both GCSE and A levels, RE is fast losing its status as a Cinderella subject. I hope that this book will act as a toolbox of ideas and activities that will help to develop teaching and learning in the subject.

*Cavan Wood*

# Curriculum ideas

**THE EMOTIONAL INTELLIGENCE APPROACH**

There are many ways in which RE can be taught through schemes of work. You can do a systematic study of a religion, or a cross-religious study of a faith experience such as pilgrimage or festivals. You can construct a scheme on a moral issue like poverty or racism.

One seldom-tried way is to examine a series of emotions and ask pupils to use the religious material to think about these issues. For example, you could look at the idea of anger. If you were using the Biblical tradition, you could examine:

> The story of Cain and Abel in Genesis, as an example of the way in which anger can be destructive
> Jonah's anger with God – anger as irrational
> Amos' anger with Israel and Judah – anger at the abuse of others
> Jesus' cleansing of the Temple, 'righteous anger'

This should encourage pupils to think through the causes and the appropriateness of anger. Alain de Botton's essay on anger in *The Consolations of Philosophy* (Penguin, 2007) is well worth a read.

Would it be possible to devise a curriculum which in part reflected some of the emotional problems/states that pupils are going through? This might further help to bridge the gap between their experiences and the relevance they think RE has for their lives.

All teachers appreciate the importance of a bright, inviting classroom which will help pupils to see the value of the subject. You can also use your classroom as a place to hold an exhibition. One approach I have tried was to give pupils the type of experience I had visiting Yad Vashem in Jerusalem. This is the museum dedicated to the memory of those murdered in the Nazi Holocaust. In the museum, there are collections of paintings done by children in the camps, photographs of those who were there and piles of items like shoes and spectacles to recall the way the Allies found these when they liberated the prisoners at the end of the Second World War.

You can log on to www.yadvashem.org, the official site of the museum. I photocopied and enlarged some of the most vivid images and stuck them up around my classroom before pupils entered. I then encouraged pupils to walk around and look in detail at the images in silence. After they had done this, I asked them to take a piece of paper and write down what they had seen in just one of the images. They were also asked to think about how this made them feel. Again, I emphasized the idea of keeping silent in order to make them think about the Holocaust.

Many pupils used their words or descriptions to turn these into a poem or an extended piece of writing. You could also provide some writing frames linked to each image as one possibility to help those who may have literacy difficulties.

Wisdom literature, such as Proverbs or Ecclesiastes in the Bible, is seldom explored. There are many other wisdom books in other religions such as the Mishnah in Judaism and the Hadith in Islam as well as the many collections within Buddhism.

Here are some wise sayings that could form the basis for discussion:

*Paradise is found at the feet of your mother.*
(The Hadith)

*The wise son hears his father's instruction, but a scoffer does not listen to instruction.* (Proverbs 13:1)

*For everything there is a season and a time for every matter under heaven.* (Ecclesiastes 3:1)

*Yoshi ben Yochanon from Jerusalem said: 'Let your home be open wide to the multitudes. Let the poor be like children of your home. And don't overemphasize light conversation with your spouse.'* (The Mishnah)

The use of stories or proverbs to illustrate and pass on ideas is of course not just limited to religion. Try to get pupils to think about how they might write their own instructions for life.

They might also like to consider how some pieces of work seem to cancel each other out, for example 'Many hands make light work' versus 'Too many cooks spoil the broth'. You could get them to think through the difference between wisdom and knowledge.

RE has increasingly been a subject where human rights issues have been addressed. Topics like the wearing of the veil, religious freedom of speech and how far the state should respect or embrace a religious issue have become live debates. Yet there are many other human rights debates that have the potential for discussion. Here are some websites you might find useful:

Christian Solidarity Worldwide at www.csw.org.uk campaigns against Christians being persecuted and seeks to put pressure on governments to help stop this.
There is a full statement from a Christian point of view on human rights at www. evangelicalsforhumanrights.org, based on Biblical teaching.
For many Christians, the issue of the death penalty is important – see the website dedicated to Sister Helen Prejean, who has worked for its abolition across the USA, at www.prejean.org.
Amnesty International has an extensive site at www. amnesty.org, and is a non-religious organization. Founded in the early 1960s by Peter Bettenson, Amnesty campaigns for both religious and non-religious prisoners of conscience.

Other faiths too are interested in human rights, for example:

Islamic Human Rights Commission at www.ihrc.org
Jewish Human Rights Network at www.jhrn.org.uk
Buddhist views on human rights at www.buddhanetz. org
Hindu Human Rights at www.hinduhumanrights.org

These sites and any others that come up on a search engine are best checked by the teacher before use in class to check for their suitability.

**ZEN SLOW WALKING**

There is a great deal that Zen Buddhism can teach pupils about the way that they look at the world. One thing you could try is to take your class outside and encourage them to walk as slowly as possible over a set distance. The natural inclination for anyone involved is to be competitive, so it will be a good calming exercise for both pupils and teacher alike. You must continually work with the group so that each footstep they take is smaller than the one they took immediately before. You could introduce this by referring to Carl Honore's book *In Praise of Slow* (Orion, 2005), which looks at various movements such as the slow food groups, who encourage people to eat in such a way that they enjoy their food rather than see it as energy that you shovel down in order to fuel up.

The slow walking could lead into a period of Buddhist meditation or to encourage pupils to think about the use of stillness or silence in various traditions, for example in Buddhist or Christian monasticism.

Pupils could also reflect on the idea 'Be still and know that I am God' from Psalm 48. Why might stillness help people find God?

Jung wrote 'Busyness isn't of the Devil: it is the Devil!' What do you think he meant? Can we avoid being rushed, and stressed as a consequence?

Food is often a vital part of religion, important for celebration or symbolic of some other truth. One method in which we all learn is by our sense of taste. We should seek to develop a sense awareness in pupils. We are good at teaching them in a way that encourages them to use sight and listening, but we ought to encourage the other senses as well.

Meals or food that could be very helpful:

A Passover reconstruction meal – there are many textbooks which give enough detail for this.
The Shabbat meal – for Judaism, it is vital to meet around a meal to worship God and also to celebrate the importance of the family.
Communion – by sharing some bread and a non-alcoholic alternative to wine (e.g. blackcurrant juice), groups can begin to understand the importance of this event to Christians. It is vital to emphasize that you are not doing the communion as in church – this is an analogous experience, not the actual one.
The gurdwara – if you cannot visit a Sikh temple, why not reconstruct one of the meals that people would be offered on entering the building.

There are other meals and food that are important, for example Haman's ears, which Jews make at Purim. If you can, try to work with the Food Technology department to help you make the food.

RECONSTRUCTION MEALS

This is an exercise designed to make pupils think about moral and religious issues. It could form the basis for a cross-curricular piece of work with Citizenship and/or English. You can do this as a writing exercise or as a role play. Pupils should work in groups of twos or threes, so that everyone can contribute something.

Imagine that you are involved in a shipwreck of a spacecraft, on another planet. Twenty people (including you) survive. Some of these people you like; others you do not like at all. Draw up a list of the twenty, who can include famous people, your friends and people with particular jobs. In order to survive, you will need to work together. Establish the following points:

Choose a leader. How will you do this? Describe a way to choose a leader.

Write a story about some of the problems the people on the planet might face about choosing their leader.

Draw and label a map of your planet, showing the key places.

Decide on some laws and rules.

Consider what punishments you might need if people decide not to follow the rules.

What problems do you think people who make our laws have? How could you overcome such problems?

If the twenty are settled on the planet for a long time, will they need to develop their own rituals and ceremonies? Would religion act as a way to bind people together?

Give reasons for your answers, showing that you have considered more than one point of view.

Introducing the idea of a creed to a group of pupils can be quite difficult. Take the example of the Apostles' Creed below – how much of this would most pupils understand?

*The Apostles' Creed*

*I believe in God, the Father Almighty, creator of heaven and earth.*

*I believe in Jesus Christ, his only Son, Our Lord.*

*He was conceived by the power of the Holy Spirit and born of the Virgin Mary.*

*He suffered under Pontius Pilate, was crucified, died and was buried.*

*He descended to the dead.*

*On the third day, he rose again.*

*He ascended into heaven and is seated at the right hand of the Father.*

*He will come again to judge the living and the dead.*

*I believe in the Holy Spirit.*

*The holy Catholic Church.*

*The communion of saints.*

*The resurrection of the body.*

*And the life everlasting.*

*Amen*

You could get pupils to highlight words or phrases in this creed that they find particularly difficult to understand, and in other statements of faith such as the Mool Mantar in Sikhism.

Many pupils may suggest that only religious people have beliefs. Why not get them to write their own creed. It could contain five statements, such as how they think people should behave ('I think people should not be racist') or what they believe about themselves or what they could accomplish. You might like to get them to think about what they worship – is it a football club, a pop star or a supermodel? You could ask them to do this as an ICT exercise.

The idea that life is sacred is one shared by many religions. This is often in conflict with many perceptions about modern science and medicine. Ask pupils to define what they mean by life. You could also ask the Science department; they often have definitions that they teach as part of the National Curriculum or GCSEs which could be useful guides. Here is a selection of sites that might help you with teaching issues on the sanctity of life:

**ABORTION-RELATED SITES**
All sites need to be viewed, and if used in school you may need to load them on to an intranet rather than allow open access.

www.lifecharity.org.uk – the major anti-abortion campaign site
www.catholic-ew.org.uk – the Roman Catholic Church's teaching on abortion explained
www.christiananswers.net – seeks to answer many questions
www.abortionrights.org.uk – the best pro-choice site for information

**EUTHANASIA**
These sites give information about the subject, not to help with it!

www.bbc.co.uk/religion/ethics/euthanasia/overview/keywords.shtml
www.bbc.co.uk/schools/gcsebitesize/biology

**CLONING**

www.ornl.gov – information about cloning and the human genome project

The idea of prophecy is seldom taught in RE in schools and yet it is a vital part of the Biblical tradition, and very important to Islam and many other faiths. If you take the Biblical understanding of prophecy, there are essentially three parts to it:

1  The criticism of culture or the world as it is. For prophets, like Muhammad or Amos, this is because they have received a message from God himself explaining the evil of the day they live in.
2  The looking forward to a time when things will be put right and all will live in peace.
3  Some encouragement or explanation on how to get there, normally a call to people to change their behaviour.

PROPHECY

Ask pupils to write down three or four things they believe to be wrong with the world. Then they should look forward to a time when these things are put right. They should also try to think about how they might be part of a process to make sure that they put these things right.

You could read extracts from prophetic books (the image of the new earth and heaven in Revelation might well inspire) or speeches like 'I Have a Dream' by Martin Luther King which are structured using Biblical material.

A good idea is to share ideas with the class as a model. For example:

I am appalled by the racism I see in the world.
I look forward to the day when people are not judged by their skin colour and we all live as one.
I can help this to happen by treating all people fairly and challenging others when they do not.

DRAWING A GRAPH

The idea of using the techniques pupils might have been used to in Science or Maths might seem strange, but drawing a graph of emotions and experience undergone might well be revealing.

On the x axis, put the events of the story of the Prodigal Son: 1. The younger son asks the father for money. 2. The younger son leaves home. 3. The younger son has a good time. 4. The younger son ends up working in a pigsty. 5. The younger son decides to return home. 6. The father sees the younger son from afar. 7. The father prepares for a party to welcome him home. 8. The elder son is angry. 9. The father tells the elder son of his love for his younger son.

On the y axis, trace three lines, one for each of the three characters. The lines should indicate whether the characters are pleased or sad or disturbed. You could put a median line where x and y meet at 90 degrees so that they have a norm line to measure the reactions to.

This graph may help pupils to plan for a piece of written work where they need to ensure that they reflect the emotions of the people involved in the story, in order to give the story more three-dimensionality.

There is a dilemma in asking pupils to write prayers of their own. Is writing a prayer an educational activity or really is it trying to encourage religious feeling? Knowing key prayers from religions is something that should be seen as an entitlement to their spiritual learning. To be aware of the Lord's Prayer or the prayer of St Francis is important, given that they are often referred to in print or in the media.

Prayers are about various activities. They include:

Confession – saying sorry for sins to God. Even the least religious of pupils can develop a piece on the idea of confession, the importance of saying sorry.

Thanksgiving – celebrating and being grateful for the good things in life. Expressing thanks is a good activity for pupils to do, even if these thanks are not necessarily directed at God. As a starter activity, you could ask them to compile a list of things or people they are thankful for.

Adoration – expressing love and devotion to God. The idea of using the language of love to someone else is a little tricky, but you could draw a comparison between the words of a hymn and a pop song about love.

Intercession – these are asking prayers, asking God to intervene to change a situation such as an illness or a need in a country. This might lead you to ask pupils how they could be the person who answers someone else's prayer. You could also use an extract from the film Bruce Almighty, which looks at how a man stands in the place of God and has to try to answer prayers.

The RE class can be a place where we can generate information which we can use in lessons. Asking fifty pupils to get two adults to fill in a simple questionnaire will enable us to know the opinions of one hundred adults in the area in which we teach. This can be used to generate pie charts, bar graphs and other mathematical ways to represent data. This may give information that could also be used in a cross-curricular project with Mathematics, Statistics or Sociology. What sort of information could we survey? Here are some possible questions for a survey that you could undertake about the theme of life after death.

1  Would you say that you are:
   a. an Atheist, b. an Agnostic,
   c. a Theist, d. a Polytheist?
2  Do you believe in an afterlife?
   a. Yes b. No c. Unsure
3  Do you believe in a heaven?
   a. Yes b. No c. Unsure
4  Do you believe in a hell?
   a. Yes b. No c. Unsure
5  Do you believe in a purgatory?
   a. Yes b. No c. Unsure
6  Do you believe in reincarnation?
   a. Yes b. No c. Unsure
7  Do you think that there is a purpose to life?
   a. Yes b. No c. Unsure

Almost any subject in the RE syllabus can be used to help compile an extensive database. This can provide information which you can use for many years after the initial survey.

Teaching about the environment is increasingly a major focus in teaching RE. There are many excellent resources in this area. The following websites/organizations are particularly helpful if you are setting a piece of work based on these issues:

Cafod, Romero Close, Stockwell Road, London, SW9 9TY. www.cafod.org.uk
Christian Aid, PO Box 100, London SE1 7RT. www.christianaid.org.uk or www.christian-aid.ie. Christian Aid has been highlighting the link between carbon emissions, climate change and the way this may lead to extreme weather conditions.
Christian Ecology Link, 3 Bond Street, Lancaster LA1 3ER. Christian Ecology Link is co-sponsor of Operation Noah, a joint campaign with the Churches Together in Britain to cut carbon emissions.

Other religious-based groups working in this area include:

the Dharma Gaia Trust at http://teknozen.igc.org/dgt/, or Earth Sangha at www.earthsangha.org/, for a Buddhist viewpoint.
Islamic Foundation for Ecology and Environmental Sciences. Email: info@ifees.org.uk. www.ifees.org.uk/. They publish a journal called *EcoIslam* and others.
The Noah Project, PO Box 1828, London W10 5RT. www.BigGreenJewish.org.uk. A Jewish organization worth exploring, The Noah Project has a very full website, with quizzes, and articles explaining Jewish ideas on the care of the earth and its life.
RE-XS, at www.re-xs.ucsm.ac.uk, will also give you other links.

This is a rapidly changing area and it is advisable that the teacher screens the sites in order to make sure that they fully explore the issues concerning the environment.

THE ENVIRONMENT

There are a number of different ways in which a teacher can introduce the theme of worship. Why not try one of these?

The Worship Sheet. Give every person – including the teacher and any other adults present – a sheet of paper. At the top, they write their own name as, for example, 'Cavan Wood is . . .' The rest of the class will then complete this sentence with a positive adjective or word that they think describes the person named on the sheet. Explain to the class that they are going to be given a few minutes to go round the room and write something positive on as many sheets as possible. If they cannot write anything positive, then they should write nothing. Make sure that before the class sits down, everybody has got at least one positive comment on their sheet. This introduces the idea of being praised and will also help build student self-image.

The Worship Chair. If you do not like the idea of the class wandering about, you could put a chair at the front of the room, which you say is the Worship Chair. Anyone who sits in it is to be praised or told encouraging things about themselves. Try to ensure that you choose the people who go in the chair. Make sure that you have an equal spread of boys and girls, those who are confident and those who may be shy. This can be very important again for introducing the idea of worship, but it also can be used to reinforce the idea that you wish your classroom to be a positive rather than a negative place.

**IDEA**

# 16

Pupils need to know about the importance of festivals to people in religions and one of the ways to do this is to get them to plan their own festival. Festivals contain a number of different ideas. Let me just take one and suggest how it could be the basis for a piece of extended work.

One of the meanings of the Passover is the idea of liberation, of freedom. Ask pupils to devise a festival that celebrates the idea of freedom. What could this mean in practice? It could be:

Freedom from fear
Freedom from debt
Freedom from oppression and bullying

Pupils should include a story about how the key narrative in the festival reflects their freedom, and a sacred set of actions that you need to carry out. For example, to celebrate freedom from past mistakes, you could write the mistakes on balloons and let them float away, as a sign that you are beginning to have a new start.

Pupils will also need to include prayers, a service, hymn or song words to reflect the festival, which can be either original or borrowed with permission. They should try to present this either in a small booklet or on an A3 wall display.

DESIGNING A FESTIVAL

17

**A VENN DIAGRAM**

The use of a Venn diagram will be familiar to Mathematics students. The RE specialist could use it to compare and contrast two different religious stories or traditions. For example, Islam and Christianity have a great deal in common and a great deal that separates them. The Venn diagram enables pupils to see these clearly. They can then begin to see areas where they personally disagree and where they coincide. This could also help weaker pupils develop their extended writing.

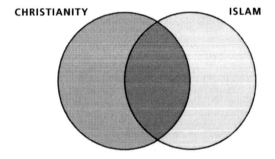

CHRISTIANITY         ISLAM

# Assessment and homework

**BINARY OPERATIONS**

Many postmodern philosophers have used the idea of binary operations – matching two contrasting words or phrases, then choosing the one that better fits what you believe (see David Harvey's *The Condition of Postmodernity* (Blackwell, 1991), which uses such a list to contrast modernism with postmodernism). You could give pupils a list of binary operations and then underline the one they think is closer to the subject. They then have to write a sentence about the subject, using their word of choice and explaining why they have chosen it. Here are some examples:

**KING DAVID**
Wise/foolish
Brave/cowardly
Noble/rude
Holy/sinful
Good father/bad father
Good husband/bad husband
Proud/humble
Loving/hateful
Straightforward/complicated
King David was wise because he realized when he had made mistakes
King David was sinful because in the story about Bathsheba, he committed adultery and organized the murder of her husband Uriah
King David was proud because he decided to take Bathsheba when he should not
King David was a complicated person because . . .

**GURU NANAK**
Wise/foolish
Peace-loving/argumentative
Uniting/dividing
Religious/non-religious
Proud/humble
Loving/hateful
Good teacher/bad teacher
Straightforward/complicated
Guru Nanak was wise because he thought for himself

Guru Nanak seemed to pick arguments because he
    thought much Hindu and Muslim tradition did
    not make any sense
Guru Nanak was a good teacher because he made
    people think

These can become the sentence stems which then
encourage pupils to write a short essay about the person
being studied. They may form the basis for a formative
assessment.

Student voice is becoming a very important way in which we can develop pupils' experience of teaching and learning. There are many ways in which you could use student voice in order to help. For example, your school could train older pupils to sit in with younger pupils' lessons, with specific focus on examining how easy or not the class found and responded to instructions given by the teacher. They are evaluating communication, not the lesson.

Another way to develop pupil voice is through the use of lesson evaluation forms, in which you ask pupils to focus on one lesson. This might be one that you have not done before or perhaps one which was not as successful as you had hoped. A third possible strategy is to have a questionnaire in which you target a selected cross-section of pupils. Try to make sure there are balances in gender, age and ability.

You may need to pilot the questionnaire with a small group before giving it to a larger number. Make sure that in the final questionnaire you have a reasonably large enough response to give accurate information, but also that you do not ask too many pupils so that it becomes impossible to really analyse what they are telling you.

When I was working on an MA, I interviewed pupils in groups of threes and fours, selecting at random those who had previously answered questionnaires. This provided me with a great deal of information and gave me a context to the results I had earlier examined.

For non-exam RE, this approach of using questionnaires could be used to devise a survey that could help you design a syllabus that meets less resistance. For pupils to think this process is important, there must be some clear changes to teaching and learning as a consequence.

Homework is one of the most stressful areas for the RE teacher, given that we see a greater number of different classes than any other type of teacher. To actively chase all the homework that we could set, if we were to set every week, would be a task in itself. We also need to think about setting homework less frequently but more effectively. Instead of setting a variety of tasks for, say, four out of six weeks in a half-term, we should aim to set one task on which we advise pupils to take a similar amount of time. We need to be able to encourage independent research and extended writing, which have often been seen as lacking in RE. The use of project-based homework will free us and will enable pupils to think through more carefully how they manage their work. It will give them adequate time get in contact with religious groups, to fully exploit the internet's resources and perhaps to make time to interview on a particular theme.

Some examples of longer-term projects could be:

Design a new church building for the twenty-first century.
Research the Punjab and its effects on shaping Sikh identity.
Design and write a magazine tackling Jesus' miracles, aimed at teenagers.

Having a longer duration will enable the majority of the pupils to try to achieve a depth and imagination which a more hurried approach will not foster. It will also help in developing our assessment of pupils as it may provide a substantial piece of work to help with levelling.

WORKING WITH OTHERS

The Working with Others project, based at the University of Brighton, is worth contacting in order to help you think through how you can create starters and plenaries that encourage pupils to work with others and not just their chosen friends or partners in a group.

To do any exercise, the project recommends that you follow the order below:

1   Start with the pre-brief. Explain clearly what the purpose of the activity is and how you would like pupils to behave, what they should be thinking about while the activity is going on and what skills they might learn through this exercise.

2   Do the activity. For example, the trust and acceptance exercises in Idea 39 would be quite useful. The project supplies other ideas for activities which can be adapted for the RE classroom.

3   End with the debriefing. The teacher brings all the class together and asks a series of questions to establish how they feel about the activity and what they may or may not have learned from it. The teacher can build upon their responses to press them to understand the importance of the activity. Questions should ideally be open-ended in order to encourage pupils' participation. The activities are specifically designed to encourage the ideas of trust and listening, so they could be very useful to illustrate the ideas behind prayer.

Contact Working with Others at: Working with Others Research and Education Unit, University of Brighton, Business Services, Mithras House, Lewes Road, Brighton BN2 4AT.

Pupils need to be involved in their own and their peers' assessment. If they are, they will probably learn something more deeply than just from teacher input. How could this be achieved? Here are some suggestions:

Pupils who have undertaken a project (e.g. Why is the gurdwara important to Sikhs?) are given a criteria sheet and mark their own project against them. They then pass this on to a partner, who does the same exercise. Finally, the teacher will use the criteria sheet for marking.

Give pupils an example of an answer to the question they may be studying from former students. You could also give a variety of answers, revealing different levels at Key Stage 3 or GCSE. Ask pupils to compare the different responses and see if they can suggest ways to write better answers.

Write your own model answers, which again reflect various grades (try A, C and E, for example, to begin with). Ask pupils to grade them and to use the criteria sheet to see where they need to add any further ideas in order to write a better answer.

Pupils can discuss whether they think that the answer given is reasonable and fits the criteria, if it is matching the title of the project or the exam question.

There are many other methods of self- and peer assessment: look on the website of the Department for Children, Schools and Families (www.dfes.gov.uk) for further information.

SELF- AND PEER ASSESSMENT

**TARGET SETTING**

It is very important that pupils should try to set their own targets as a result of the peer and self-assessment exercises that were discussed in Idea 22. We may need to give them some clues as to how they could improve. Areas for consideration include:

To make sure that they use religious language precisely and effectively.

To show that they know that in a religious tradition there can be a variety of understandings of a particular teaching or story.

To show clearly the diversity of belief and practice within and between religions. For example, pupils should naturally use phrases such as 'some' or 'most' when talking about members of a religion's beliefs, never saying an absolute statement such as 'All Christians believe that abortion is murder'.

To be able to argue coherently, and with understanding, two different points of view when asked to do so.

To write with appropriate detail for the task set.

Pupils will probably come up with a good many more, but try to make sure that the targets they set themselves are ones that they can realistically obtain and also contain some element of challenge/difficulty.

Encourage pupils to consider how they might make the journey from one level to another, possibly with a series of smaller achievable steps in the meantime.

Make sure that targets are recorded and are re-examined on a regular basis in order to see if they have been achieved.

# Outside help

If you are going to have speakers from faith communities in school, it is vital to make visits run smoothly. An ill-thought-out visit may greatly harm and limit pupils' understanding and reinforce negative stereotypes.

Here are some suggestions you may like to follow when inviting a speaker into school:

Meet speakers before they come to your school. Talk to them and get to know what makes them tick. Make sure that speakers are well briefed on why they are there; if they are there to talk about their faith, they should be informed that they must not speak in a way that puts pressure on pupils to come to the same decisions as they have. There is nothing more embarrassing than a visitor who decides to preach. Make sure that speakers can present their ideas in a way that builds on pupil understanding, and that if they use technical words, these are fully explained in a constructive way.

WELCOMING SPEAKERS TO SCHOOLS

Museums, both local and national, can provide a vital resource for RE. The British Museum is a superb centre to find many things linked with many of the world's religions. The British Library has a great collection of sacred books. Yet as well as the artefacts of a religion that you might find in such museums, think too about the other opportunities museums can bring.

The Imperial War Museum has an excellent range of exhibitions, everything from the Holocaust to the Blitz experience, to coverage of more recent conflicts. This should help to reinforce the pupils' understanding of war, helping them to see it as more than just a philosophical problem about the correctness of fighting.

Other museums to which a visit is worth considering include the Natural History Museum, which could introduce pupils to the idea of the complexity of the world. You could use it as a way to deepen the debate about the idea of creation and whether it has to be in conflict with modern science.

Similarly, the Science Museum may well help pupils gain a sense of the complexity and wonder of the universe. Scientist Johannes Kepler once said that, for him, science was 'thinking God's thoughts after him'.

Seemingly secular museums can be valuable in that they encourage pupils to ask a whole series of ultimate or moral questions in a context that may make it easier for some of them to see the relevance to their own life.

VISITING MUSEUMS

Many religions have set up museums in which they can show and help to explain their faiths. One very good example of this is The Jewish Museum based at 34 Upper Berkeley Street, London W1H 5AU. The museum is willing to offer interactive educational resources tailored for pupils in Key Stages 1 to 5. Opportunities on offer include a focus on festivals and a synagogue tour as well as teaching about the Holocaust appropriate for each age group.

Other good museums include the Islamic Cultural Centre, which can be contacted at The Islamic Cultural Centre, 146 Park Road, London NW8 7RG. This museum is attached to the Regent's Park Mosque.

There are many others from different faiths that you will be able to find across the country, via the internet or through local knowledge. What is vital is that the teacher visits the museum before the pupils' visit to make sure that it is of a good standard and is appropriate in its depiction of the faith it represents. Although museums will often supply educational resources, it may be necessary to modify these and make sure that they are pupil-friendly.

Try to find a possible guide for the museum and talk through the particular objectives you might have for a visit to the establishment.

# Starters and plenaries

**IDEA**

# 27

BINGO

The key words of a lesson can be reinforced by playing Bingo with pupils. If you have an interactive whiteboard, make sure that the key words will appear onscreen in order to help pupils fill in the Bingo grid. It is important that every pupil gets a grid and that the game is played at great speed. You might like to think about how you would reward the first person to shout 'House'. You could alter 'House' to the name of the holy building of the religion that you are studying, as a way to remind pupils.

If you were doing a lesson on Sikhism, for example, words could include guru, gurdwara, Mool Mantar and Waheguru. You would need to develop clues as triggers to identify each of the key terms, for example 'The Sikh holy building', or clues to reward more advanced pupils, for example 'The gate of the Guru' (both of these are clues for the gurdwara). If pupils become confident doing this, you could select a group to devise a Bingo game as part of their own learning during the lesson.

Pupils could use these words to create a crossword on the theme of the lesson and they should try to include four words from the lesson which have not appeared in the Bingo game grid.

Alternatively, they could make sure that they do a piece of writing that includes all the key words mentioned in the game.

You might like to try this as a way to assess pupils. They can sometimes answer direct questions in a test (e.g. How many plagues were there?) but not fully understand the story and any abstract ideas within it.

Do any of these words go together? Link them with a line and write a sentence explaining what the connection is. You may connect a word more than once to another.

CONCEPT MAPPING

| | |
|---|---|
| MOSES | PASSOVER |
| EGYPT | LIBERATION |
| SLAVERY | ANGEL OF DEATH |
| PLAGUES | MIRACLE |

WHO WANTS TO BE A MILLIONAIRE?

Using the format of the programme *Who Wants to Be a Millionaire?*, a good plenary can be developed. Remember the format of the questions: there have to be four possible options. Here is an example for Guru Nanak:

When Guru Nanak was born, what did his parents see around his body?

a. A golden circle of light
b. A purple circle of light
c. A blue circle of light
d. A red circle of light.

(Answer: a.)

In order to play this properly, you will need to have eight to ten questions prepared. Try to make sure that there is a time limit. Also, tell the rest of the class that shouting out will not be tolerated at any point.

Make sure that you seek one or two contestants. They can do the following if they want help:

Ask the audience – put the options to a hand vote and then the contestants decide which option to take.
Fifty/fifty – reduce the options down to two, one of which is the right answer.
Ask a friend – rather than phone one, they must suggest the name of a friend they will ask if they get stuck on the questions.

If you have access to a whiteboard, try to use it to make the event more dramatic. You might like to think through whether or not you will be awarding a prize for any winning contestants.

GUIDED FANTASY

Getting pupils to use their imagination doesn't always mean that they need to produce a piece of written work or a drawing! One way in which to engage with them could be through the idea of guided fantasy.

Ask all pupils to be quiet and close their eyes. The stillness is vital to making the exercise work. You then read or relate a fantasy which they can get to grips with. Here are a couple of examples:

**THE MOST IMPORTANT THING**

Imagine that you have arrived home. Go in through the door and make your way through the house to where your bedroom is. Sit on your bed and look around. What do you see? Try to find in your imagination the one thing in the room that you would have to save in a fire. (This is designed to help develop a lesson on worship.)

**FEAR**

Imagine that you are sitting on the floor in a room with a few other people. You are all feeling afraid. There is one window through which a breeze is blowing. Gradually, this becomes louder and more intense. Then in the room there is a feeling of heat. Then everybody in the room gets up and dances; they are unafraid. (This is focused on Pentecost.)

Too many pupils have received images from other sources such as DVDs and TV – the guided fantasy approach will help get that brain muscle working!

KIM'S GAME

Kim's Game is a memory game which gets its name from the novel *Kim* by Rudyard Kipling, in which the title character is taught to observe very small details and remember them.

Kim's Game is a party favourite which can be adapted to help develop recall. Take a tray and put onto it things that link to the topic of the lesson and then cover the tray, asking pupils to write down as many items as they can. For example, this could be used for the story of the Passover and the Seder meal, such as a lamb bone, a matzo and horseradish.

After covering the tray, you could give pupils a list, which they need to check against the items they have seen. For example, you could do a list on Passover, and add an Easter Egg or a hot cross bun to help them realize which items belong to which religion, and this will hopefully stop them from confusing different faiths.

Also, you could list definitions of the items on the tray and get the pupils to work out from these what the item is, for example 'What stands for the sacrifice made on Passover night?' (Answer: the lamb bone).

You could compile on a sheet a mixture of images and words. Pupils either have to write the word linked to the item, or have to draw the item from the given word.

One possibility for a starter or plenary is to use a diamond-ranking exercise. Pupils are given a number of different statements which they have to rank either in importance or by closer/further away from their own point of view. This is best done first in groups of three or four debating the pros and cons of the variety of statements, and then with a whiteboard or with a large photocopied version of the statements visible to pupils.

You might like to try this exercise based on the idea of miracles:

Miracles are misunderstandings of natural events.
Miracles break the laws of nature and therefore cannot happen.
Miracles suspend the laws of nature and do happen.
Miracles happen all the time, such as the sun coming up.
Miracles are unique events caused by God.
Miracle stories are all made up or exaggerated.
Most people never see a miracle, therefore they do not exist.
If God can do miracles, why doesn't He choose to do more, given the problems in the world?
Miracles are not caused by God – they are coincidences or luck.

This will enable pupils to develop their critical thinking skills and their ability to argue. They could then select the strongest and the weakest argument as they see it and write a paragraph either in support or in opposition to each.

This can be repeated for many other topics.

DIAMOND-RANKING EXERCISE

It is important that we make sure that pupils are given challenges in RE lessons. Using a crossword can be a good activity for plenaries or starters, as a way to convey the important words in the lesson. There are internet sites which will enable you to put in clues and to make it, for example www.puzzlemaker. Crosswords are preferable to word searches as they demand pupils think a great deal more about their answers.

You could also work the puzzle the other way round by filling in the answers and then asking pupils to devise questions to define them. You could use the clues to help add to the definitions or ideas that pupils have of key words. Here are some examples:

Islamic holy journey (5) (Answer: Hajji)
Sikh teacher (4) (Answer: guru)
Act of God or breaking the law of nature? (7)
(Answer: miracle)
Hindu place of worship attracts a male (6)
(Answer: mandir)

Consider what clues you might devise for the following words:

Sikh
Mosque
Jesus
Hinduism
Covenant
Monotheism

You could also make sure that the words taken together reveal a paragraph that summarizes the lesson's topic, with pupils having to add in their own conjunctions. Pupils who tend to finish quickly could even help you by devising the crossword on puzzlemaker, but check that they use the appropriate words and that they spell them correctly.

One very successful plenary is based on the TV quiz show *Blockbusters*. This could consist of two rounds. In the first, you just have one letter for the clues. In the second and more difficult round – known as the Gold Run – you have two letters. This works on using initials of key ideas and asking a set of questions to find out what each means. Here is an example based on the life of Muhammad:

MU – prophet of Islam (Muhammad)
KH – wife of a prophet (Khadijah)
KIM – building in holy city (Kaaba in Makkah)
AJ – heavenly being sent with message for Muhammad (Angel Jibril)
MH – place where the prophet received a vision (Mount Hira)
Q – Holy book of Islam (The Qur'an)
POI – important acts in the religion of Muhammad (Five pillars of Islam)
COM – place Muhammad had to flee from Makkah (City of Madinah)
RE – a vision given by God (Revelation)
AL – Muslim name for God (Allah)
KAIM – Holy building in Makkah (The Kaaba in Makkah)

The clues should be challenging so that it is not easy to immediately complete a Gold Run across the board. The game can easily be played on whiteboards. You can also develop a board in which you can fit any initials for any other topic that you choose to use.

**IDEA 34**

**BLOCKBUSTERS**

**HOT SEATING**

The idea of hot seating builds upon the use of interviewing techniques. Put a chair at the front of the classroom and tell the pupils that is where a religious figure will be interviewed. There are a couple of ways you could do this.

Let us consider an idea from Sikhism. Tell pupils the story of Guru Nanak or one particular story connected with him. Students should then be asked to compose three questions they might ask him if they were able to interview him. The teacher then plays the role of the guru and the pupil can have a supplementary question if necessary.

An alternative is to give pupils the information and get them to prepare a set of questions for one member of the group to be the person interviewed.

While this will work with many faith traditions, you must be careful not to offend: an interview with Muhammad is not wise, as it does not fit the Islamic views on the representation of human beings. There are some basic rules that you need to follow:

Brief students to think about how the religious person might think in their day, not as they might think today.
Make sure that all the questions are sensible and reflect the areas studied.

Allow time for feedback on how this mini-role play could be improved.

Pupils are often keen to share their opinions. Yet sometimes we ask them to express themselves in ways in which they might not be comfortable, as that isn't the normal way they communicate. We need to use methods they can relate to.

You could try this. Find some large pieces of sugar paper or an old blanket and put these up on a wall. In the centre, write a focus such as 'To me God is . . .', and then invite pupils to add to this by either writing a few words or contributing some images which relate to the theme. Tell them that they must stick to the theme.

You then have a display as a potential reference point for a scheme of work, and could even build upon pupils' contributions. Some other starting sentences are:

Life is sacred so . . .

War is . . .

Religion is . . .

Sex should be . . .

If Jesus/Guru Nanak/Buddha/Muhammad were here today he would . . .

The Bible is . . .

Illustration below – on the theme of war. Include the following:

War is . . .

- necessary
- a waste
- evil
- needless
- nothing to do with God
- caused by religion
- sometimes moral
- caused by selfishness
- due to violence in humans

**THE GRAFFITI WALL**

Hangman is a game that most pupils should be familiar with. You might encourage them to think about the key words or phrases used in the lesson and to ask them to put up their clues to challenge the class. Alternatively, you can write a set of your own to reinforce the meanings and key terms of the lesson.

The key terms from the lesson are gradually revealed on the board. If you were doing a lesson on an introduction to Islam, words and phrases might include:

> Islam
> Muhammad
> Makkah
> Prophet
> Allah
> Five pillars of Islam
> Saudi Arabia
> The Kaaba
> The Qur'an
> Ignorance

Try to include as many pupils as possible. It is important to include terms that might relate to the story, not only technical terms, but also emotions or ideas that are key to the topic that has been studied.

Make sure that pupils have accurately spelt the words they are going to use, or else the class may find themselves frustrated! Once all of the words have been solved, pupils could write them down in their book with a definition or a sentence to explain each of the ones chosen. Alternatively, terms could be used as the basis for a piece of extended writing or for an exercise such as writing a postcard (see Idea 60) or a poem.

Here are some ideas for quick plenaries:

RE Shootout. This is a game you can play with pupils who are particularly active. Ask the class to stand. Explain that you will point your hand at someone as if you are about to shoot them. Point, and ask one pupil a question. If the pupil gets it right, he or she can ask six other people to sit down, although that pupil must remain standing. If the pupil gets it wrong, he or she has to sit down alone. Carry on until you only have two people standing and then ask them questions until only one person is left standing, having answered all the questions correctly.

Thumbs up. Ask pupils to put thumbs up for something they have understood, thumbs down for something they have not understood and thumbs horizontal if they have not yet fully understood it.

Post-it notes. Arrange to have a board at the front of your classroom. Before the end of the lesson, give out a post-it note upon which you will ask the pupils to write, and to complete the following sentence: 'One thing I have learned in this lesson is . . .' or 'One thing that I need to work on is . . .'

Good plenaries will be well planned and thoughtful; they will be built into the structure of the lesson.

QUICK PLENARIES

**TRUST AND ACCEPTANCE**

One idea that is at the heart of religion is the idea of trust or faith. One way to show the importance of this is through a trust and acceptance game. Here are two examples:

1. Sheep and Shepherd. Blindfold a group of pupils (this is best done outside if you can!) and put them in an area where they have to move across from one end to another. They can only do this successfully by listening to the instructions from the shepherd. Obviously, this can be used to explain or develop themes in Psalm 23 or Jesus' claim to be 'the good shepherd'.

2. Faith and Trust Circle. Ask a pupil to stand in the centre of a circle, to close his or her eyes and fall backwards. The people in the circle should then gently move the pupil about, making sure that he or she is safe and not roughly handled. If you are feeling brave, you might like to take a turn in the centre and see how far you can trust the pupils to keep you safe!

These exercises should be fruitful if used with the right pupils. Some questions that might result from these are:

Did you feel you could trust other people to keep you safe?

How might closing your eyes be like trusting in God?

Is it harder to believe in something you cannot see?

Or does it make no difference?

PAPER PLANES

One of the banes of the RE teacher's life is the badly thrown paper plane. Why not turn things on their head by using their interest in making them to your advantage?

Give all pupils a piece of paper. At the front or on the whiteboard, show how you wish them to make a plane. On the inside of the plane, they must write a question. They will then fly their plane in the direction of another pupil and the pupil who receives it must try to answer the question posed.

Topics could include:

What question would you like to ask Jesus/ Muhammad/another religious leader?
What question would you like to ask God?
Why do you think there is evil in the world?
Why do you think there is suffering in the world?
Do you think science disproves religion?
What one thing do you think people could do to begin to make the world a better place?

The key thing is to ensure that you do this with a group who will clearly follow the instructions that you give them on how to do it. Also, use sparingly; only the brave should attempt it when being observed by Ofsted or your senior management!

# IDEA
# 41

## STATUS AND IMPORTANCE

One recurring theme in RE is that of status and importance. Be it the position one should keep the Qur'an in a room to show it respect or the Christian idea of God sending his Son into the world and surrendering power, the theme is often there. Pupils need to be able to find an analogous experience to understand about status and power and to think through what these concepts mean.

One way is a theatre game on status and focus first used by Augusto Boal. Here is a variation for RE. Using six chairs, a table and a book, the group move the objects around until they can agree on what has the highest status. Then you go on to include pupils, who are told to adopt particular positions such as standing tall or lying on the floor. The status of the pupils relative to the objects is then assigned. Status can be defined by many things in the world. It may be the connections a person has ('I am the Son of God'), or about wealth or personal charisma, or the ability to hold people's attention. When you consider religious leaders, few of them had much traditional power or status – Jesus is born to a poor family, Muhammad and Guru Nanak have modest beginnings. Only the Buddha is born into power as a prince, but he only really gains status and authority when he has given all of this up in order to find the truth.

The discussions emerging from the exercise should enable pupils to think through the issues on status in religion and in the world.

The idea behind traffic lights is to be able to give pupils and teachers an indication of how far the teaching has been effective. This is part of the move towards assessment for learning, which encourages pupils to think carefully about their own development.

Red – this is a way of saying that the pupil has not understood the content of the lesson and needs urgent help to reach the required level.

Amber – this suggests that the pupil feels that the majority of the lesson was explicable but there are elements that need to be clarified.

Green – this suggests that the pupil feels fully confident that he or she understands all the lesson content and feels that he or she will be able to explain it.

You may wish to give pupils red, amber and green cards, or you can give them a sheet with the illustration of traffic lights above.

You could also have cards that say 'Yes', 'No' and 'Unsure' if you would prefer that.

**TRAFFIC LIGHTS**

# Cross-curricular links

**ASSEMBLIES**

Many RE teachers find that they are asked to lead or organize collective worships. Some feel that this will inevitably lead to a conflict with the work that they are doing in their classrooms. This does not have to be case. It can be a place where the more experimental elements that you might be doing in lessons can be celebrated and shared with the rest of the school.

Good assemblies can follow many different types, and companion volumes *100 Ideas for Assemblies: Primary School Edition* and *100 Ideas for Secondary School Assemblies* can provide you with many ideas. There are many other excellent resources, such as Assembly File (Optioning Education), which can be ordered to help you. The case should be that if you are going to do assembly, do it well! Perhaps unfairly, RE can often be judged by the quality of assemblies in school and sometimes you will find yourself having to explain that the way religious material is used does not always match the way it has been used. Non-specialists can often misuse key stories to make them fit with a general appeal, for example to stop throwing litter in the playground.

You will need to make sure that any assemblies that you lead will show the religious context of any story or belief, then apply them to the life and experience of those listening. The two most powerful ways to do this are either by a storytelling approach or by the use of striking images, perhaps by using PowerPoint.

Make sure that if you conduct assemblies that they are remembered by the pupils for the right reasons!

RE teachers need to ensure that the presence of the subject is helping to develop school life as a whole. While RE staff are often asked to contribute through assemblies and to teach PSHE, there is also a responsibility to work with colleagues.

So where might RE help or lead?

India week. RE could encourage collaboration with the History and Geography departments on a themed week or day about India. Food Technology could add a 'Taste of India'. The Dance and Drama departments could look at Hindu dance. English could examine literature that covers the experiences of people who lived in India or were influenced by it.

Human rights, human wrongs. RE could take the lead in a week on the theme of human rights by putting on an exhibition related to the Holocaust, perhaps of pupil work or the travelling exhibitions that some Jewish groups might supply.

The Forgiveness project. If you look at www. theforgivenessproject.com, you will find a rich source of stories about the idea of forgiveness. This could be used as a way into talking about Easter and the Christian idea of forgiveness as shown in the Cross and Resurrection. It could form the basis of a week of activities with PSHE, Drama and Art.

Islam awareness week. Many pupils have developed Islamaphobic attitudes and it is important that we should help to counter stereotypes. This could give the opportunity to work with Maths and Science with regards to Islamic science and medicine, as well as Art on Islamic design.

CROSS-CURRICULAR WEEKS 1

Here are a few more suggestions for cross-curricular weeks:

Martin Luther King. King's life is celebrated in many US states on the Monday closest to 15 January, his birthday. Why not arrange a week of activities based on this? Dance or Drama could produce some movement based on his speeches. English could look at how he used the power of words to make his points. RE should study in depth the root of his Christian thinking, which is often neglected or underplayed by History.

Artefacts. Work with Technology and Art to look at the artefacts of religions. Why not get pupils to have a go at making stained glass or designing a mezuzah?

Other religions, other cultures. It might be a good idea to work with Modern Languages to see if it is possible to develop teaching about the experience of religion in the areas they look at.

A guidebook to local faith. Work with the ICT department to encourage pupils to compile a guidebook to the places of worship in your area.

Faith in music. Work with the Music department to look at the music of faiths. You could put on some workshops to look at the different types, from Gospel to the Sikh singing in a gurdwara.

Encouraging pupils to develop a newspaper article about a religious theme is one way in which they can think through some of the issues on bias and interpretation in religion. It is important to set a task to help pupils develop a whole set of competing versions. After all, the four gospels each give us an account of the Resurrection of Jesus, but are in many respects very different about the details. The writings of Josephus (the Jewish historian just after the time of Jesus) or those of Pliny (a Roman historian) could be used to help pupils understand the different viewpoints of the period. Pupils could be asked to do the following:

Create a name for your paper.
Write a bold headline.
When writing about the Resurrection, make sure that you report the views of the Christians, the Romans and the Jews. Show a variety of opinions.
You could write an editorial for your newspaper, trying to look at all the evidence and the opinions about the Resurrection, coming to your own conclusions as to what happened.

The use of Word might help pupils to create the typeface that looks like a newspaper. Using Google images or other picture search engines will also help pupils to develop an impressive piece of work. With clear planning, creating a newspaper on a religious theme should help to develop a critical thinking approach which will help prepare or develop pupils for GCSE.

WRITING NEWSPAPER ARTICLES

CITIZENSHIP

RE is a subject that can help to deliver a great deal of the Citizenship agenda. It will naturally include reference to development issues, prejudice, war, the environment and multicultural awareness. There are other ways that we can contribute to this subject, for example in assemblies (see Idea 43) and cross-curricular themed weeks or days (see Idea 44).

Other ways to strengthen the link include:

Ensuring that faith communities contribute to assemblies, encouraging them to talk about both their beliefs and how these might affect the wider community

Featuring religious news on any Citizenship board, both local and international.

Make sure that religion is shown in a positive light.

Pupils undertaking Citizenship coursework have the possibility of working with a religious group, helping the homeless or a development charity.

You could help arrange a 'Question Time' with local politicians and make sure that your pupils ask questions that reflect not only political issues but also broader moral questions.

We should be encouraging pupils to think critically about the society around them, using material from religious education. Politicians may well like the idea of Citizenship as they feel that it may make pupils more willing participants in democracy. We should encourage them to be critical friends!

It is important that RE teachers remember that every child has an appropriate curriculum. Howard Gardner's work on multiple intelligences has been key to developing approaches on teaching and learning. These include:

Linguistic intelligence.

Musical intelligence.

Logical-mathematical intelligence. How far are children with this type of intelligence served by RE?

Spatial intelligence.

Bodily kinaesthetic intelligence. How far do we allow children who are particularly gifted in sport or skills that require moving about to flourish in our classrooms?

Personal intelligences. These are especially useful to RE, as they include a pupil's ability to be able to empathize with others.

This list is not exhaustive; visual and auditory learners need to be taken into account. There have been studies looking at gender differences; does your curriculum reflect subject matter likely to interest males and females? Do you think about how boys and girls might have different approaches to learning?

Differentiation should not just be about perceived academic intelligence; we need to make sure that we reflect on all the factors we can in order to make the learning experience as successful as possible. As the majority of pupils have limited personal experience of religion, we should ensure that they are taught in such a way that they are involved. Emphasis needs to include 'Learning about' (the facts, beliefs, information of religion) and 'Learning from' (the individuals' responses to these and the life questions they may provoke).

# Writing approaches

A recent question in a GCSE Short Course paper asked: ' "War, what is it good for – absolutely nothing!" What might a Christian say to this? What do you think, giving reasons for your answer. Show that you have thought about it from two different points of view.'

The quotation is from a 1960s song but was used in an exam in 2002! Many pupils would have been unaware of the source. Would they have written better answers if they had seen the whole lyric?

Song lyrics can sometimes have an immediacy, an emotion and a familiarity for pupils that poems might not. Pop songs can convey powerful messages and looking at their lyrics can be a way into analysing religious and moral issues.

If you are going to look at lyrics, make sure of the following:

All pupils have access to the lyrics, to ensure they can understand them.

Cut out unnecessary repetition in the original like repeated words or verses that may make it a good record but which may distract pupils.

Choose lyrics that are appropriate to the topic.

Make sure you understand the context of the lyric, especially if there is possible ambiguity in meaning.

Make sure that the lyric really fits your lesson objective. Any doubts, then do not use it. It could be a distraction, not something to help develop understanding.

Consider whether it would be a good idea or not to play the record. Unless you give some warning, pupils can be very resistant to musical styles that are not their favourites.

Writing poetry can be an excellent way to develop pupils' empathy with religious feelings and ideas.

You may need to model to pupils how to write poems. Why not use hymns, religious songs and poems as examples and ask them to write their version (see Idea 51). Poems do not have to rhyme (see Idea 56) but can express truth in different way to prose.

You could provide pupils with a first line and possibly even a last line to cover the topic. More able students can be challenged by asking them to write more challenging forms such as a sonnet (fourteen lines) or some kind of acrostic, using either the alphabet or a particular word from a religion. As long as you can keep them focused, you might even try to get some pupils to attempt to write a limerick.

Most pupils will now be familiar with one particular type of poetry – rap. Pupils can use rap in RE, but you must make sure that they do not use racist, sexist, homophobic or obscene language or ideas. Most pupils think they know the structures to writing a rap; only a few can do so successfully, but when it is done correctly, then it can produce work which is both fun and educational. Make sure too that they do more than pastiche their favourite rap track and try to develop their own work. Many stories do have a recurring structure which can lend itself to this form, such as the parables of Jesus.

**WRITING A PSALM**

It is important to introduce pupils to various types of religious literature. One of the most important forms in the Biblical tradition is the psalm. Why not make a study of psalms part of a module on the Bible? It is important that the Bible transmits ideas not only via stories but also through the very personal songs and poems the psalms represent. They reflect a variety of events and emotions: there are psalms about how you feel when friends have betrayed you, and about how as a nation you deal with things when you are defeated in battle. Many are very personal, about how the person who wrote them is feeling towards God. Walter Brueggemann suggests that many psalms follow a pattern:

1 Orientation – they were written at a particular point and describe what the moment was about, for example 'By the rivers of Babylon, we sat down and wept . . .'
2 Disorientation – they go on to explain why the psalmist is unhappy or feels far from God.
3 Re-orientation – they go on to praise God or seek to find meaning in and from difficult moments.

Try to use some different recordings of psalms, such as U2's '40', which is on their 'War' album, or 'Rivers of Babylon' by Boney M as well as the more traditional hymn versions of Psalm 23.

Pupils' activity: Write a modern-day psalm. Try to make it fit the pattern of Walter Brueggemann: explaining where a person is, saying why he or she might be feeling unhappy or far from God and then how this person might find meaning in the experience and hope for the future.

Looking at various quotations set out in the chapter and verse layout that the world's sacred scriptures use can often be difficult for pupils to engage with. One alternative is to make a selection of quotations on a piece of paper. You could cut and paste a choice of quotations from religious leaders such as the Pope or Muhammad, which may give pupils a sense of the overall teaching of the person. You can also use these to create discussion by focusing on a theme. If you were doing a scheme of work on money, you could include many different traditions, but do not assign them to begin with, to encourage pupils to see how similar they can be. Here are some examples:

> A man is more than his possessions. (Jesus)
> The love of money is the root of all kinds of evil. (Paul)
> Set not your hearts on another's possessions. (Hinduism)
> Money answers all things. (Ecclesiastes)

Ideally, you should have eight to ten quotations on the sheet and you must make sure that pupils discuss all of them. They could work in small groups and, taking one of the quotations, they could devise a presentation, perhaps using PowerPoint to show the beliefs they think the statement is trying to put across and the implications of how people might then live their lives.

QUOTATION SHEETS

**WRITING FRAMES**

Literacy is a key skill in developing a pupil's understanding of religion. As RE consists in part of looking at metaphors and similes, and reflecting on the power of stories, encouraging literacy has to be a priority.

Writing frames are one way forward. Here are a couple of suggestions. You could present the class with a sheet with some of the words in the text missing and they simply have to insert them. They may well be able to do this, as it is probably not the most taxing of exercises! You could leave words blank and they have to try to think of the appropriate insertion! This will encourage them to think. Using textbooks, in particular, or encouraging pupils to develop extended pieces of writing, or sentence stems, which you then ask them to develop into an essay, might help them enormously to be able to write as you want them to. Here is one example - war and peace:

You are to write an essay on the religious understanding of war and peace. Here is the essay structure:

1 There are many reasons why wars are fought. These include . . . (try to think through and explain in detail at least five reasons).
2 There are many consequences to war. These include . . .
3 Some Christians believe in the Just War Theory. This is the belief that sometimes it is better to fight than not to. The reasons they give for this include . . .
4 Some Christians are pacifists. They base their opposition to war on . . .
5 Muslims too have different ideas about war. These include . . .
6 I agree/disagree that fighting in a war will help solve problems in the world. I think this because . . .

Some pupils can be encouraged to develop empathy for a character by asking them to write in the guise of the person studied. This is not advisable when studying Islam, and some other religious groups might find it difficult, so the teacher should be sensitive to the class they are teaching. The stories of both Guru Nanak and Buddha give an obvious place for autobiographical writing. Some focused questions might help pupils to write in their personas, for example:

What problems did the religious leader face and how were these tackled?
What emotions did the religious leader go through at the beginning of teaching?
How did the leader encourage and develop a group of followers to listen and spread the message?
What compelled the leader to carry on when things might have got difficult?
What successes did the leader think were achieved? Could more have been done?

One particular type of autobiographical writing might be very useful: the diary. Some pupils might even be able to produce a blog online, but check before this goes live that there is nothing in there that could be considered offensive by members of a faith. The blog might give the pupils the opportunity to include pictures and photographs which might make them more vivid.

WRITING AN AUTOBIOGRAPHY

Storytelling is a vital art for a teacher to master and needs to be constantly reviewed. You need to consider how to put across a story in a way that is appropriate to the age group. One book you will very helpful is *Anyone Can Tell a Story* by Bob Hartman (Lion, 2002). Hartman is mainly a teller of Biblical stories and traditional moral tales, but his techniques are applicable to stories from other cultures and religions. His advice for potential storytellers includes:

Build a relationship with the audience.
Find a way into the story which links with them.
Keep storytelling devices simple.
Don't talk down.
Be yourself.
Be confident.
Be friendly.
Identify with the characters in the story.
Maintain the pace and tension.
Participation is the key to building involvement with the story.

Stories are very important means of communicating ideas and beliefs in a religion. There are other ways to involve pupils in retelling stories such as through plays and role plays. Although you can use humour, be careful when you use it. This will make many pupils engage with the story, but remember that some will know the stories better than you and you will need to make sure that you tell them accurately and in a way that does not offend other people. Another useful book is *Story* by Robert McKee (Methuen, 1999), which, although written for potential scriptwriters, is very helpful in looking at how to develop storytelling.

A haiku is a form of poem which was devised by the Japanese. It is an attempt to simplify poetry and to cut to the heart of the matter. This is reflected in the Zen Buddhist belief that truth was simple and could be expressed in a simple uncomplicated poetic form.

To express something simply is a challenge that many pupils will enjoy and it may also help them to develop an understanding of the topic. You will need to introduce the rules of writing a haiku. The poem contains three lines. The first line has five syllables, the second seven and the third five. There can be variations, but it is probably best to get pupils to follow these rules at the beginning. Haiku have often focused on an abstract emotion, nature or the passing of the seasons and have therefore proved effective in showing the idea that life can be very short indeed.

Here is one example from Basho, a famous Japanese poet:

First winter shower
you can just call me
a traveller now

While you could get pupils to use this form to explore Buddhism, you could also use it to explore other faiths. Here is one example based on Christianity by the monk Anthony Hanson:

Humbled when I see
I cannot love God unless
I love you also

When you look on the internet, you should be able to find other examples of religious people who use the haiku to put across their ideas.

WRITING A BLURB

A blurb can be a piece of writing that you find on the flap or the back of a book which tries to summarize the main parts of the text in a few words. You need to encourage pupils to find the most important parts of a story in order to create a dramatic summary. How about this example of the Prodigal Son:

*A tale of rebellion, a lost son and a forgiving father, the Prodigal Son is a story which will touch the reader. The dilemmas of a son down on his luck, a father desperate to find his missing son alive and an elder brother who does not feel appreciated. Will any of the three men see their dreams come true or will they live as incomplete people? Read on and find out.*

*What the critics say:*

*'An outrageous, shocking tale of God's love.'*
*A disciple*

*'The sort of story that has given Jesus a bad name.'*
*A Pharisee*

The best blurbs both summarize the tale and tell something about how people have received the story. Here are a few other topics you could suggest:

The Good Samaritan
The life of Abraham
The life of Moses
Guru Gobind Singh: a biography

This is also a good way to help pupils to see that the majority of religious material has ended up in a book, but that to begin with, the majority of the stories were told orally.

One way to introduce a story to pupils is by a series of cards with the key parts of the story on them which are randomly sorted. In small groups, the cards must be rearranged to make sure that the right order is established. This will encourage pupils to think about the importance of the story as a whole and may well aid the concentration of the group. Here is an example: the story of Lazarus and the rich man. Try to see how long it takes you to rearrange the tale into the right order.

1   But Abraham replied, 'If they didn't listen to Moses and to the prophets, they won't listen to man coming back from the dead.'
2   'Father Abraham, let Lazarus go back to warn my brothers,' said the rich man.
3   There was a rich man who lived in luxury while a poor man called Lazarus sat at his gate. One day, the beggar died and he went to be with Abraham in heaven.
4   The rich man begged Abraham to send Lazarus back to earth to warn his five brothers not to be as foolish as he had been.
5   The rich man died and was taken to hell. He looked up to Lazarus in heaven. He saw Abraham beside the poor man and asked Abraham to help him escape the place of suffering.

CUT-UP STORY

WRITING SCRIPTED INTERVIEWS

While some pupils will be relaxed about the idea of hot seating (see Idea 35), not all will feel comfortable with this. So why not get pupils to script an interview?

Ask them to think about the way a chat show on television works: a principal interviewer and two or more guests. For example, you could have a chat show featuring Jesus, a Pharisee and a disciple. In the last chapters of Matthew there are many stories on Jesus being subjected to cross-examination and it should therefore be easy to transfer some of this material.

Here is an example of how one scene might go:

Interviewer: My first guest began life in a stable and now has a preaching ministry which has taken him all over the country. Let us give a warm welcome to Jesus of Nazareth.

Jesus: Thank you for inviting me. Many people often do not want to listen to what I say.

Interviewer: Why do you think they might be like that? Do you think that perhaps you are too controversial about the way that you deal with the important issues you believe in?

Jesus: I said on one occasion that I had come to bring a sword, not peace.

Interviewer: You see, it is that kind of language which can anger and upset people.

Jesus: Truth can upset. But if you know the truth, it can also set you free.

You could use this as the start and get pupils to develop it from this point.

To encourage pupils' writing, we will sometimes need to take small steps in order to help them build up confidence. As you can normally fit only a small number of words onto the back of a postcard, this can be an ideal way to introduce writing on issues to précis important ideas. Tell the pupils that they have precisely fifty words to describe an event or idea (excluding the 'Dear . . .' greeting at the beginning and the 'Yours, so and so' at the end). You could provide them with plain white postcards, encouraging them to draw a symbol or picture that reflects the content of what they write about on the other side.

Examples of what you could use the technique for include:

What a person might find on a visit to a holy place such as a church or mosque
The meaning of some important religious symbol(s), for example the 5 Ks of Sikhism, or ideas such as the Trinity, Creation and Incarnation in Christianity.

Alternatively, you could ask them to do this as an email, but still limit the number of words. If there are a few pupils who think they could do it by text, then allow them to do so, but make it clear that this should be written in a way to cover as much as possible and as close to spoken English as possible.

WRITING A POSTCARD FROM . . . .

**LETTERS AND EMAILS**

Letter writing can be a very important way of communication. Within Christianity, the letters of Paul and the other epistle writers as well as the Encyclicals of the Pope have had an enormous impact on how believers think and act. Letters also help pupils to empathize with others. You could try to do the following:

What would Paul write today? Work with a group to think about the issues a modern-day Paul might want to highlight and then ask them to write in his persona.
A letter to God. Young children's letters to God have proved to be very popular with publishers and this technique of asking pupils to write to God might help them to reveal some interesting questions they might ask or their views about the Being.
Using 1 Corinthians 13 on love, ask pupils to write a letter from one Christian to another which shows the importance of this concept, perhaps imagining a situation where the Christian idea of love needs to be lived out in practice.

Some classes may be much more comfortable using email. Ask the class if they think that emails and letters achieve different aims. Can you say things in letters that you cannot in emails and vice versa? Do letters have a longer-term effect than emails? How might religious people use email effectively?

There are many ways in which newspaper articles can be used, for example as a provocative starter to a lesson, or linking an ongoing moral debate such as abortion or war with a headline modern story. The RE-XS website will help you to access the sites of several tabloids and broadsheets (see Idea 87 for further information). Looking at the ways in which newspapers cover the same story, with their different perspectives and biases, is a good introduction to learning about how worldviews shape what is supposed to be objective. Different newspapers covering the same story might also help pupils to understand how the synoptic gospels can have different understandings or emphases on the same events. This should be able to show that even if evidence is not uniform, it is still important to use the different versions of the story to build our understanding of what exactly is going on.

This technique will be especially valuable when examining the accounts of the Resurrection. Pupils could also use Venn diagrams (see Idea 17) to see overlaps and differences between the four gospel versions of the events.

Regular use of newspapers will also contribute to the development of pupils' ability to think in ways as suggested by the Citizenship curriculum and could help develop an approach where more able pupils in particular follow the GCSE short courses in both Religious Studies and Citizenship.

## MODERN RETELLING OF STORIES

One way of making connections with pupils is to use books or films that draw upon religious stories. John Steinbeck's *East of Eden* (Penguin, 2001) is an example of the Cain and Abel narrative; why not compare an extract with the story in Genesis 3? Thomas Mann's novel *Joseph and His Brothers* (Everyman's Library, 2005) and the pop operetta *Joseph and the Amazing Technicolor Dreamcoat* are good sources on the Joseph story you will find in Genesis, but they both have significant limitations in the retelling. Asking pupils to research a story and to compare/contrast the ways in which it is retold is quite important, as this can make them aware of the potential difficulties in doing it. When you look at some Biblical stories, for example, they are often without the detail pupils might assume: the wise men are not named in the Matthew version of the birth of Jesus and there are not three of them! Sometimes people think that motives are imputed to characters that are not necessarily there. For example, Bathsheba did not consciously lead David into adultery: there is no evidence in the biblical text to support that she was being manipulative. Indeed, it suggested that David is at fault due to his attitude. Yet novels, films or stories being retold can give us insight and they can be useful.

One of the experiences that schools do not often prepare people for is death, either their own or that of a loved one. Religious Education looks at the idea of the sanctity of life or the ideas that religions have about life after death or about reincarnation/birth. Gerard Hughes in his book *God of Surprises* (Darton, Longman & Todd, 1996) suggests that as a spiritual exercise, people should write their own obituary to help them think about what the meaning of their lives should be and what they wish to achieve.

You could use this in two ways:

1 Ask pupils to do as Hughes suggested. Then ask those who will be willing to read out what they have written. Ask one of the group to write down on the board any ideas that seem to recur. Talk about what makes a life worth living. How might religion influence this?

2 Write a biography of a religious figure. In a limited number of words – say 250 – pupils have to try to catch the essence of the person's life and teaching. This is a good exercise to help them focus on the most important aspects of a person. You can then ask pupils to read these out and see if there are common threads or obvious omissions. For example, does an obituary of Jesus explain the ideas his disciples have about his rising from the dead or is it too narrowly focused on his moral teaching?

WRITING AN OBITUARY

**THE FIVE Ws**

This approach to making pupils think through an issue was inspired by a Rudyard Kipling poem, which referred to servants who could help you understand the reality of the world around you. There are five key words that you can apply to the work you wish pupils to undertake:

1 What?
2 Where?
3 Who?
4 When?
5 Why?

These have been used to help pupils think through issues. Let us look at an example based on the miracles of Jesus:

1 What? What do we mean by a miracle?
2 Where? Where in time and place are miracles more/less likely to take place?
3 Who? Who is responsible for the miracle? Can it be explained by the presence of Jesus or another divine being?
4 When? When did it happen? What conditions made it happen? Could they apply in today's world?
5 Why? Why did these events happen? Why may they not happen or happen less frequently than in the time of Jesus?

You could also put these words by the side of a photograph or a picture in order to stimulate their thoughts. This can be applied to many other subjects, and to the following topics:

The birth of Guru Nanak
The career of the Prophet Muhammad
The start of the Church in the first century

# The Arts

**GAME MAKING**

Snakes and Ladders was reputedly developed by Hindus keen to explain the idea of reincarnation. Game making can be a summary exercise or possible assessment method. The *Skills Challenge* books by Terence Copley and Adrian Brown (Religious and Moral Education Press, 1993, 1995) include ready-to-use games that have been tested on pupils. Another approach is to encourage pupils to develop games themselves. You will need to set out a few criteria to make sure that the game making achieves educational aims rather than just a way to grab pupils' interest or to avoid having to teach them directly!

Any good game should have:

A well-designed board which reflects the theme
A set of questions related to the area of study
A series of options cards to explore the story/teaching

Here is an example, called The Buddha Game, which I created for Year 9 pupils studying Buddhism. They also have to write a short report, which can be given to the people who made the game as a way of encouraging self- and peer assessment.

### THE BUDDHA GAME

*You will create a board game which explores the key ideas of Buddhism. The aim of the game is to reach nirvana, in which you escape from rebirth and suffering. You will need to include:*

> *The four encounters that shaped the Buddha – the old man, the ill man, the dead man and the holy man*
> *The Four Noble Truths*
> *The Eightfold Path*
> *Nirvana, karma and re-birth*

*Your game should also include the following:*
> *Question cards on Buddhism*
> *Penalty cards relating to Buddhist teaching, for example 'You have failed to remember the First Noble Truth'*
> *Plus cards – where you are able to advance across the board quickly as you have succeeded in getting more knowledge about Buddhism*

*Counters*
*You will need to make a pair of dice*

*You have [insert a number] hours of homework and it should be handed in on [insert date].*

COLLAGE

Collage has been called a postmodern art form, in that it draws upon existing materials which it can then remove from their context in order to give them new meaning. How might pupils use collage in RE? They can of course use today's images to retell a parable or the life story of a religious figure. They could try to shoehorn into their collages not just what a person looks or looked like but the spirit of that person. Think for a moment about how the personality of Jesus could be displayed in a collage without actually using any representation of him. You might want to use images that suggest a person who challenges authority, has wisdom and is sacrificed for a higher cause. Or you could do a collage that looked at the consequences of a person's life. One devoted to Martin Luther King could show the ideas behind the speech 'I Have a Dream' or his final speech, 'The Promised Land'. Collages can of course also be used for forming representations; if you can, collect a variety of images from Google or another search engine, which can be very helpful (see Idea 69). They can show the key idea of a religion or a religious text: 1 Corinthians 13 on love could be the basis for a good collage, as could Galatians 5 on Paul's list of the fruit of the spirit.

Symbols are important to religions, as they can address key ideas in a faith without having to use words. Yet they can also become devalued: one popular urban myth has a young girl returning a crucifix to a shop as she wanted one 'with that little man on it'. Challenge pupils to look at the basics of a religion and see if they can find an image or a potential symbol that could replace the traditional one. Most traditions have a principal image (in Christianity, the Cross) and a variety of secondary symbols (such as the dove, the fish or the chalice).

Then tell them that they should try to devise an original symbol that must show something of importance to the faith. If you talk about love and sacrifice as key to the Christian message, what might the symbol be? If Islam seems to feel that submission and devotion is a key message, how might that be shown?

Should the new symbol be something that appeals to the computer generation, rather than a static image on a piece of paper? If you can, get access to a computer suite to help pupils to do this. You could have members of the faith communities examine these new symbols and choose a winner that they think best expresses the key ideas of their beliefs.

RESPONSES TO IMAGES

We live increasingly in a world of images and their power, so it is vital that we teach our pupils how to 'read' an image for ideas. This will be useful to them in more than RE; teenagers can sometimes be very uncritical of the images they are presented with and what these might be trying to convey.

Give pupils two different images of religious leaders such as Guru Nanak and Jesus Christ to reflect on, then give them a series of questions:

How did artists know what these people looked like?
How can the pictures be used as evidence to support belief in Guru Nanak or Jesus?
Are the pictures shaped by the artists' own beliefs about the religious leader?
How might you show these figures if you were going to draw them or make a three-dimensional image such as a sculpture?

Obviously, this could form the basis for a cross-curricular project with the Art department; before trying this, it might be a good idea to ask them how they might go about the exercise. Focus on how religious ideas are conveyed or shaped by artists' or believers' images or work. Pupils could use Google or another search engine to find more images of leaders and then select from these a wider range which they personally like and dislike.

Ask pupils to devise a image of Jesus or the Buddha that shows their importance today as well as drawing upon traditional representation. The Buddhist monastery run by Thai monks in Wimbledon has one wall where the Buddha is seen both meeting the Queen, near a double-decker bus, and talking to a punk, as their way to show his relevance to the UK.

Posters can often be used when a teacher has got struck and finding ideas on them can be one way to set class- and homework. In RE, we should use posters from religious organizations or with religious content as teaching aids. Pupils need to be able to think critically about the messages these might present. They should be introduced to the idea that, by their nature, posters often simplify ideas or use vivid images to shock or stimulate. Pupils should be offered models of poster work from previous classes as well as given the opportunity to look at commercially or professionally produced examples.

Some suggestions to improve posters:

Make sure that the poster covers the theme of the lesson. Pupils often wish to put irrelevant images to reflect their interests, which don't always match the topic.

Ask pupils to look at each other's work and offer suggestions as to how others could improve what they are producing.

Consider if this should be a task to be done by ICT.

Posters should respect religious sensitivities. For example, any poster connected with Islam should not have human faces on it, especially of Muhammad or an image of Allah.

Give a clear brief either in writing or on the whiteboard of exactly what you want the pupils to achieve.

Ask yourself these questions: Is a poster the best way of presenting it? How far is it developing pupils' understanding?

**CREATION – IMAGES OF OURSELVES**

One of the important teachings in many religions is creation and with that normally comes a belief about human beings. For Christians, this is often expressed as 'being in the image of God'. In other faiths, there may be an emphasis on humans being the children of God.

How could you explore this? The theatre theorist Augusto Boal suggests that we carry around with us an unconscious image of how we see ourselves, which often governs how we behave. He believes that by unlocking this image humans can alter their own views. One way to do this is to get pieces of A2 sized paper and ask pupils to lie on them. Give each a pencil and tell them to sit up and with their eyes closed draw their body shape. Then ask them to hold these up and discuss what the image looks like, what it might seem to tell us about the person.

Next read a passage like this one:

> *Then God said, 'Let us make man in our image, in our likeness, and let them rule over the fish of the sea and the birds of the air, over the livestock, over all the earth, and over all the creatures that move along the ground.'*
> *So God created man in his own image, in the image of God he created him; male and female he created them.*
> (Genesis 1:27–8, New International Version)

Now ask pupils to redraw their image, but having in mind this belief that they are special. Does this alter the two images?

It is important that every RE classroom has pupil-produced work for encouragement and positive support.

Look again at the symbols of the six major world religions in Idea 68. Give pupils at least two pieces of homework to produce a mobile that could be hung from the ceiling. They should use at least one of these symbols (they may use all of them) and may use other religious symbols they know (e.g. a fish as a symbol for Christianity). If they wish to use other religious symbols, they should consult the teacher before going ahead.

These are handed in to the teacher upon completion, which would be a good time to allow pupils to assess the most successful mobiles. Some criteria include:

How accurate are the images of the faiths represented in the mobile?
How well designed is the mobile?
Is there an appropriate use of colour?
Does the mobile reflect careful planning?

You might like to consult with colleagues in Design and Technology in order to help reinforce skills in design, planning and making. They may be able to give you some practical ideas to make this exercise easier for pupils, who might be able to adapt it to help them complete some of the tasks they have undertaken in the National Curriculum. Make sure too that mobiles are regularly replaced by others, as they do attract wear and tear!

A MOBILE

MIME AND MOVEMENT

Why not try to get pupils to think through the meaning of a passage of a holy book by asking them to devise a series of movements? Look at the quotations below from Isaiah – how might you get pupils to create a mime or series of movements to go with this?

*The Spirit of the Sovereign LORD is on me,*
*because the LORD has anointed me*
*to preach good news to the poor.*
*He has sent me to bind up the brokenhearted,*
*to proclaim freedom for the captives*
*and release from darkness for the prisoners,*
*to proclaim the year of the LORD's favour*
*and the day of vengeance of our God,*
*to comfort all who mourn, and provide for those who*
*    grieve in Zion –*
*to bestow on them a crown of beauty*
*instead of ashes,*
*the oil of gladness*
*instead of mourning,*
*and a garment of praise*
*instead of a spirit of despair.*
*They will be called oaks of righteousness,*
*a planting of the LORD*
*for the display of his splendour.*
    (Isaiah 61:1-3, New International Version)

You might have to start by carefully going through the text to pick out key words that pupils might not understand so that barriers can be overcome.

The movements could be done in unison as a group or individuals could take part. This should be relatively cringe-free for pupils who might not find it easy to speak in class.

You could also use other material such as the Apostles' Creed, the Lord's Prayer or the Mool Mantar from Sikhism.

The use of drama in RE is a good opportunity to involve all pupils. If you have the confidence, and if appropriate, why not write a playlet about a religious leader? You could ask a GCSE group to put together a piece of drama to perform to a Key Stage 3 class, which might explore an issue or a story which they are examining. Observation of a Drama class may also help you think through how to use it in your lessons. Ask the teacher about the ground rules and the advice given to classes in order to make sure that when pupils come to your class they have a consistency of approach.

DRAMA

Make sure that if your playlet deals with a religious leader that pupils are told clearly not to 'put on' an accent. A play about Guru Nanak does not benefit from a cod Bengali and may well be offensive to some pupils.

Read through any existing play/sketch a couple of times to make sure that the language is appropriate and the depiction of the religious content/person is accurate. Make sure that if you do use existing scripts that the copyright issues are observed.

If you write one, make sure that you try to have as many parts as possible, varying in length, so that you can attempt to include as many pupils as possible.

Music is of primary importance to most religious traditions and one way to teach RE is to introduce the different styles of music used by religions. Try to get the various different types on a CD. Pupils may have heard gospel music, but have they heard plainsong, Buddhist chanting or the Songs of the Sufis? As part of their education, they should be made aware of the many different cultural forms in which worship can be carried out. After giving pupils examples, try to encourage them to create their own version of the music they have heard or to work together to create a musical form that expresses their culture. You might also like to begin to collect musical instruments that might have an important part in the worship of others. A lesson about Yom Kippur will be more powerful and involve pupils more if the shofar (the ram's horn) can be blown as part of the lesson, to help pupils become aware of the sound that calls people to repentance. You can easily find instruments in places like Oxfam, which often stock them as trinkets.

Ask pupils why they think music is so powerful. Does music need lyrics in order to have power or does the power rest in the tune? Why do they feel that some religious people think that music is an inappropriate means to create worship?

Pupils can be great researchers and can find out a great deal that the teacher might not have access to. We are all consumers of media and one way to help develop the relevance in RE is for pupils to keep a media diary on a particular theme. You could focus on a specific topic, for example the ways that women are depicted in the media, or on a more general task, for example the number and type of mentions on religion in the media used. You can also ask pupils to record and evaluate the images as positive, negative or neutral. Below is a template to help you.

| MEDIA DIARY | POSITIVE | NEGATIVE | NEUTRAL |
|---|---|---|---|
| MONDAY | | | |
| TUESDAY | | | |
| WEDNESDAY | | | |
| THURSDAY | | | |
| FRIDAY | | | |
| SATURDAY | | | |
| SUNDAY | | | |

Pupils should use as many different types of media as possible, and should list them in order to achieve a wide coverage, for example DVDs, videos, film, television, radio, CDs/downloads, websites, emails received, video games, newspapers, magazines and books.

By asking pupils to sift images into positive, negative and neutral, you should be able to have an informed discussion about the issues. This is suitable homework for more than one Key Stage. Emphasize to pupils that what you want is significant information, so some days may record little to the theme they are researching and others will be packed with details.

Role play demands a degree of planning in order to make sure that it does not turn into a waste of time and effort. The best way is to make sure that any role play is precisely defined. For example, if you were going to do a lesson on abortion, then you would need to provide a great deal of information before giving pupils specific characters. Here is one suggestion:

*Situation: A House of Commons committee is meeting to decide whether to limit the weeks' limit on abortion from 24 to 20 weeks. Among the witnesses called are:*

*A single woman. Her boyfriend has left her and she believes that she should have the right to an abortion when she wants one.*
*A member of the LIFE campaign. This organization believes that abortion is always wrong and will do all they can to stop it legally.*
*A Labour MP. This MP is from Liverpool and is a Catholic. He is pro-abortion but cautious about what should change, for fear of upsetting his voters.*
*A Methodist minister. He believes that no woman enters into an abortion easily, that it may be the lesser of two evils. He is a member of the National Abortion Campaign, which tries to protect and extend a woman's right to choose.*

There are many other characters you could include – this is just a sample! Ask pupils to work in pairs and produce a two-minute speech. You will act as a chair, trying to ask questions of all the contributors.

One way to help pupils realize the importance of religious events is to ask them to make cards or use these to analyse messages they might communicate. Ask the class to bring in a Christmas card that they have received. You can produce very quickly a series of A2 sized posters of images from old Christmas cards.

The range of pictures – from the classical to the crass – will help any class to understand a great deal about the festival as experienced by the faithful and how such events can be secularized.

You can make an interesting comparison with these cards and ones that may be sent for Eid or for Diwali. Look at artefacts such as Advent calendars – these have recently encouraged the Muslim community to adapt them as Ramadan calendars. Encourage pupils to develop cards for a religion, being aware of the sensitivities of the members of that faith. Think through what the message could be from:

One member of the faith to another
Someone who is not a follower to a member of the faith

Make them think too about how they can ensure that the images used reflect the values of the faith but communicated in a modern way. You could always design an e-card.

CARD MAKING

STAINED-GLASS WINDOWS

For centuries, the Christian Church has used stained-glass windows as a way to make their faith understandable to those who found reading difficult. By the use of bright colours, they were also able to celebrate the wonder of God. Why not get pupils to do something analogous?

Glass is not advisable. Use a piece of black sugar paper, and a stencil of a stained-glass set of panels – you can find this at www.storyboardtoys.com. There are many other web pages on stained glass and if you are near Ely, you could arrange a visit to the Stained Glass Museum attached to Ely Cathedral, perhaps as a joint trip with the Art, History or Technology departments.

The window template can be blown up to a better size. Cut out the template and then create appropriate designs using brightly coloured tissue paper. These could subsequently be stuck onto windows.

There is no reason why such stained-glass windows cannot be adapted to show other faith stories. Remember, however, that this might be a particular problem with the Muslim faith.

These windows, if made well, will be a valuable teaching resource for many years after they are first produced and the brilliance of colour may well help to make for a much brighter learning atmosphere.

Advertising is now so much a part of our culture that it can prove a useful exercise to get pupils to arrange a series of activities that could promote some aspect of faith. Look at the adverts put together by the Alpha Course (who try to encourage people to attend meetings about Christian faith) or World Vision (who organize Third World relief).

A good advertising campaign should include:

A script for a radio advert
A storyboard for a video campaign
A mailshot
A pre-paid return envelope
A poster campaign
A web page

This gives an opportunity to organize pupils into groups, bringing together those who have artistic skills with those who are better at ICT or writing. There will also be pupils willing to put on presentations using PowerPoint or to act out the adverts. Topics could include:

Trying to encourage people to attend church
Tackling Islamaphobia
The work of a faith-based charity
A moral issue that involves religious people, such as racism or nuclear weapons
Helping people to understand Sikhism or Judaism

You can also use this to get pupils to think about whether the morality of people of faith will affect the way that they put an advertising campaign together.

AN ADVERTISING CAMPAIGN

STORYBOARDS AND PHOTOMONTAGE

For RE teachers, drawing cartoon strips has been a staple for years. But why not try to develop this a little more and give it a spin? Films are storyboarded before a single scene is shot – detailed preliminary drawings and annotations are the order of the day. There are some excellent websites to help you create templates for storyboarding, such as www.youthlearn.org or www.exposure.co.uk.

If your school has a Media Studies department, ask them about their approach and put together instructions for pupils which will challenge them in terms of RE and this skill.

You could create your own storyboard of pictures and text but jumble up the images, so that pupils have to put them in order. Alternatively, you could supply some pictures and some text, so that they are creating pictures in some places and creating text in others.

Another way this could be created is to get pupils to use a digital camera and dress up in appropriate dress to supply images. Or you could get them to retell an old story in the form you might see in a girls' magazine, complete with thought bubbles!

# Creating your own INSET

NATRE

It is very important to join a professional association and the specialist group for RE is no exception, as RE teachers can often feel powerless. NATRE (the National Association for Teachers of Religious Education) is the subject teacher association for RE professionals throughout education, providing a focal point for their concerns, a representative voice at national level and publications and courses to promote professional development. They seek to address the real concerns of RE teachers in all schools and institutions, working in several ways, including:

Publication of the professional journal *REsource*. This has articles on good classroom practice, opinion on the subject and reviews of current resources.

NATRE also produces the *British Journal for Religious Education*, which looks at detailed research in areas of interest.

Courses on important issues such as assessment for learning.

Support to local teachers' groups.

An up-to-date website containing news and downloadable resources.

Lobbying functions: to monitor government action and inaction with regard to RE and responses to consultation papers; to press the case for more time, staff, training and money for RE.

NATRE can be contacted at RE Today Services. Tel: 0121 472 4242. Fax: 0121 472 7575. Email: retoday@ retoday.org.uk.

CULHAM INSTITUTE

The Culham Institute is a development and research organization working in the areas of RE, collective worship and church schools. Founded in 1980 from the closure of a teacher-training college, its work focuses on policy and promotional issues, curriculum resource development and teacher support, with a particular emphasis on the use of multimedia and ICT. It has an extensive website which every RE teacher ought to have as a favourite on their computer.

Culham Institute's training commitment is shown in a special annual training event. The St Gabriel's Programme, RE Teacher Weekend is a national and residential conference for 200 primary RE coordinators and secondary RE specialists. It is free to those who have not attended before; a small charge is made for returning attendees.

Culham Institute also administers a researchers' fund. The trust gives grants of up to £1,000 to practising Anglicans who are pursuing personal study, or undertaking projects or research relating principally to RE in schools. Consideration is given only to applicants who live or work in the Diocese of Oxford. The annual closing date for applications is 31 March.

THE FARMINGTON TRUST

The Farmington Trust was founded by the late Robert Wills in order to assist the teaching of RE in schools. This has developed into a highly regarded organization that has paid for and helped teachers to set up sabbaticals, with the intention of pursuing some study away from the classroom. As Farmington covers the costs of supply cover, this has made it possible for many in both primary and secondary school to be given time to think, read, reflect and develop new approaches to RE.

Successful applicants can opt for residential and full-time study for one term at a number of different colleges and universities with which the trust works, or for certain days or extended periods out of school without taking full leave. Those who work with Farmington are expected to give their findings in a written report and to attend the trust's conference in June or July at Harris Manchester College, Oxford, where they are asked to present a précis of their research.

The Farmington Trust also runs a website at www. farmington.ac.uk, where the full reports of previous research projects can be found. Previous topics include boys and RE, teaching RE using *The Simpsons* and teaching the Bible in a postmodern society. Even if you feel that you cannot take time out of school, this website is worth reading as it is one of the very best for ideas and information, written by practising teachers.

There are a number of organizations prepared to give funding to projects which look at the teaching and learning of pupils. The Westhill Endowment is a charity that gives grants of about £300,000 a year to those who seek to change society through education in a 'broadly Christian' manner. They are particularly interested in the work of the SACRE (Standing Committee for Religious Education – a committee in each authority that supervises the implementation of local syllabuses) in developing RE. The endowment can be contacted via their website at www.westhilltrust.org.

The Farmington Trust (see Idea 84) helps with the development of projects and provides opportunities for teachers to meet. The Links page on their website lists a large number of other educational charities, including contact details and further information.

CURRICULUM DEVELOPMENT FUNDING

**IDEA**

# 86

Starting in the early 1970s and attracting more than 15,000 people over August Bank Holiday weekend, the Greenbelt Arts Festival is an event worth knowing about for an RE teacher. The bold might feel they could take a group to it. The event is held at Cheltenham racecourse in Gloucestershire. The weekend has its origins in Evangelical Christianity, but has developed interests in the arts and in politics as well as other social and cultural issues. Designed to be an event for all the family, it includes many different varieties of music and entertainment. What it would prove to any group of pupils who attended it is that religions do not have to be dull, narrow or joyless. The festival's regularly updated website, at www.greenbelt.org.uk, gives information on some of the activities that take place.

By taking a group there, you might just help them to question many commonly held assumptions about the way Christians live their lives or think about the world around them. The festival has also been instrumental in developing new forms of worship which are more inclusive and relevant to young people.

Pupils could undertake a study of the festival to see how far it is fulfilling its aim of trying to communicate the ideas of Jesus Christ. They could develop their own advertising campaign to promote the event to their age group, highlighting aspects from existing materials that would do this.

One of the very best RE websites is RE-XS, at www.re-xs.ucsm.ac.uk. This has extensive connections to websites that are useful to both pupils and teachers alike. You will find the following on it:

World religions. You will find information on the six main world religions on the following topics: texts, art, pilgrimage, buildings, rites of passage, community and ultimate questions. The site also contains some links to non-religious belief systems such as humanism as well as the newer religious movements such as Mormonism.

News service. This provides links to six national newspapers, both broadsheets and tabloids.

Teacher's cupboard. This provides resources such as lesson plans and connections to important information such as the QCA schemes of work.

Ethical and moral issues. This has a wide range of information, from abortion to animal rights and from euthanasia to the environment. There is a great deal of material on religious responses to terrorism and war, and every moral and ethical issue featured in the GCSE syllabuses.

What's new. This provides a pathway to essential ideas and practices which the teacher needs.

The site is run by St Martin's College, which is now part of the University of Cumbria, and gives information about the PGCE courses in RE.

# Information sources

**CHRISTIAN INFORMATION SOURCES**

There are many Christian organizations and mosques which can provide the teacher with material. Here are a few websites and addresses of contacts which will help develop the teaching of Christianity.

Catholic Truth Society, 38–40 Eccleston Square, London SW1Y 1PD

Quakers (The Religious Society of Friends), Friends House, Euston Road, London NW1 2BJ

Church of England Board of Social Responsibility, Church House, Dean's Yard, London SW1P 2NZ

The Methodist Church: www.methodist.org.uk

The United Reform Church: www.urc.com

The Orthodox Church: www.britishorthodox.org

Lourdes – a vital resource if pupils are looking at miracle stories: www.lourdes-france.com

Worth Abbey – this website may give pupils an insight into life in the monastery: www.worthabbey.com

The Lord's Day Observance Society – this website will help pupils understand why Christians see Sunday as special: www.lordsday.co.uk

An excellent provider of Christian and Biblical resources: The Stapleford Centre, The Old Lace Mill, Frederick Road, Stapleford, Nottingham NG9 8FN. The centre has a catalogue of resources and provides INSET on RE, collective worship and spiritual and moral education. They also administer the Jerusalem Trust, which makes grants of up to £500 to help schools buy Christian-based resources

There are many Muslim organizations and mosques which can provide the teacher with material. Here are a few websites and addresses of contacts which will help develop the teaching of Islam.

The Regent's Park Mosque can be visited in central London: www.islamicculturalcentre.co.uk.
One of the best websites for material on Islam is www.realislam.com, which has a great deal of information that is presented in a fresh way.
Also useful are www.bbc.co.uk.religion/islam and www.bbc.co.uk.religion/islamicfestivals.
If you are researching art in Islam, try http://bmag.org.uk/artislam, which has many pictures of interest.
One key organization is the Muslim Council: MCB, PO Box 57330, London E1 2WJ. Email: admin@mcb.org.uk. It tries to represent a broad spectrum of Muslim opinion, often quoted by the media when there is a controversy about Islam.

Most local mosques are pleased to welcome groups to have a look around. Make sure that all pupils are appropriately dressed. Remember too the Muslim Museum (see Idea 26).

ISLAMIC INFORMATION SOURCES

**JUDAISM INFORMATION SOURCES**

There are many Jewish organizations and synagogues which can provide the teacher with material. Here are a few websites and addresses of contacts which will help develop the teaching of Judaism.

Board of Deputies, the group that has represented the views of The Jewish Community since 1760: www.bod.org.uk.

Another good source of information about the Jewish faith is www.aje.org.uk, the agency for Jewish Education. The Jewish Museum (see Idea 26) has a website which has selected other Jewish museums and places of interest in this country.

One of the best places to take pupils to understand the Holocaust is the Beth Shalom Holocaust Centre: The Holocaust Centre, Laxton, Newark, Nottinghamshire NG22 0PA. Tel 01623 836 627. Fax: 01623 836 647. Email office@bethshalom.com. Internationally, the website of Yad Vashem, the Holocaust Museum in Jerusalem, is an excellent resource: http://yad-vashem.org.il.

Similarly, the Anne Frank Museum in Amsterdam has an extensive collection of material that will help pupils understand what it must have been like to be a Jewish teenager in a Nazi-occupied country: www.annefrank.org. There are many other excellent sites devoted to Anne Frank which are worth using with pupils. A DVD about Anne Frank's life can be ordered from the museum.

Many local synagogues have their own websites. They are keen to have visitors. Make sure that you are aware of any dress code they would like you and your pupils to follow.

There are many Hindu organizations and mosques which can provide the teacher with material. Here are a few websites and addresses of contacts which will help develop the teaching of Hinduism.

The website www.hinduwebsite is an extensive selection of resources and information about Hinduism. You might also like to contact www. hinducouncil.uk.org, a group which represents many Hindus in this country. A site devoted to Hindu youth is www.hyuk.org, which helps pupils to understand the world of young Hindus in Britain.
One of the best known British Hindu places of worship is the Hindu Temple in Neasden: BAPS Shri Swaminarayan Mandi, 105–119 Brentfield Road, Neasden, London NW10 8LD. Tel: 020 8965 2651. Fax: 020 8965 6313. Email: info@mandir.org. Another possible contact is the International Society for Krishna Consciousness: www.iskcon.org.uk. Visit the website for information on visiting temples in London, Newcastle and elsewhere.

There are many other sites dedicated to Hinduism, so use them selectively as they often have an agenda, wanting to preach their version of the faith. (This is true of all faith sites!)

hinduwebsite.com

**HINDU INFORMATION SOURCES**

**BUDDHIST INFORMATION SOURCES**

There are many Buddhist organizations and temples which can provide the teacher with material. Here are a few websites and addresses of contacts which will help develop the teaching of Buddhism.

The very best website is www.buddhanet.net, which has good access to many addresses and resources. Other good sites include the London Buddhist Centre: www.lbc.org.uk, and http://bentrem.sycks.net, which has many links. Teaching resources can be found at http://teaching-buddhism.tripod.com. Of the many Buddhist monasteries that can be contacted, one of the best prepared for visitors is: Cittaviveka, Chithurst Buddhist Monastery, Chithurst (W. Sussex), Petersfield, Hampshire GU31 5EU. Tel: 01730 814 986. Fax: 01730 817 334. Office hours to contact for a visit: Mon, Wed and Sat: 07.00–08.00 am, Tue and Thur: 10.00 am–1.00 pm. Cittaviveka does not have a public email address; for enquiries on visits, write directly to the address above.

Please note that many monasteries have retreats which mean that visiting during these periods is not allowed.

There are many Sikh organizations and gurdwaras which can provide the teacher with material. Here are a few websites and addresses of contacts which will help develop the teaching of Sikhism.

A major source of information about the Sikh faith: www.sikh.org.

A good basic introduction to the faith: www.bbc.co.uk/religion/sikhism.

This site includes material from the Sikh holy writings, the Guru Granth Sahib: www.srigurugranthsahib.org.

A Sikh Wikipedia which looks at all the topics of importance to Sikh believers: www.sikhiwiki.org.

A valuable source for information: Sikh Missionary Society UK, 10 Featherstone Road, Southall, Middlesex UB2 5AA. Tel: 020 8574 1902. Email: info@sikhmissionarysociety.org. They produce many excellent booklets as well as running an outstanding website. Southall, where they are based, is also home to the biggest gurdwara in Europe as well as many others which are keen to welcome visitors. The Sri Guru Singh Sabha, Southall is very amenable to school visits.

Films on the Sikh community that are useful include *Bend It Like Beckham*, which looks at issues of sexual roles, racism, marriage/love and football(!) from pupils' points of view.

SIKH INFORMATION SOURCES

Increasingly, RE will be expected to deliver material about minority religions, not just the six major faiths on which RE has traditionally focused. (Non-religious ideas such as Humanism and Atheism are dealt with in Idea 95.) It may be highly unlikely that for some of these faiths you will definitely be able to find a speaker, so you may well be dependent on DVDs, books and websites. These include:

The Bahá'ís: www.bahai.org. The official site of the Bahá'ís, with extensive details.

Jainism: www.iamjain.org. A good site which explains what is like to be a Jain today.

Shinto: www.bbc.co.uk/religion/shinto. A very good straightforward account.

Confucianism: www.religioustolerance.org/confucianism. A very accessible site which gives a good account of the Chinese religion.

Rastafarianism: www.bbc.co.uk/religion/rastafari. This will give you the basic facts on the religion. You can also use http://rastafari.online.com as well as sites dedicated to Bob Marley.

Increasingly, teachers of RE have been encouraged to remember that Humanism and Atheism are beliefs and should be referred to as part of the RE curriculum. Contemporary atheists such as Richard Dawkins have their own websites, where they express their views. (see www.RichardDawkins.net). His writing and that of Christopher Hitchens in *God Is Not Great* (Atlantic, 2007) can provide useful sources for argument and reflection! One valuable contact to help you is the British Humanist Association, 1 Gower Street, London WC1E 6HD. Tel: 020 7079 3580. Fax: 020 7079 3588. www.humanism.org.uk.

Humanism is an approach to life based on humanity and reason – humanists recognize that moral values are properly founded on human nature and experience alone. Their decisions are based on the available evidence and our assessment of the outcomes of our actions, not on any belief or holy book.

The BHA is the foremost provider of humanist and non-religious ceremonies in England and Wales. They train and support a network of officiants, who provide help and information to all those interested in humanist namings, weddings and funeral services. and provide booklets, CDs and DVDs to explain their ideas.

Another valuable resource is www.positiveatheism, which contains profiles and quotations from the writings of famous atheists and sceptics.

ATHEIST AND AGNOSTIC MATERIAL

ARTEFACTS

Religions, like other facets of human culture, have a great deal of items that help believers. Be it icons in a Greek Orthodox Church, a Khalsa Sikh wearing the 5 Ks, or murtis in Hinduism, artefacts are very important. They should therefore be part of our teaching.

Pupils should be able to touch items, in order to get a sense of their importance. They must be encouraged to handle them appropriately and by doing this, they will learn the respect that believers have for them. The best way is to build up year by year a collection, themed by religion in boxes. When you visit an area known for its multi-religious nature, try to spend some of the department's money on items.

Try to avoid the obviously kitsch, such as the notorious pictures of Jesus where he appears to wink at you while hanging on the Cross. Items do not have to be expensive, but ought to try to be tasteful. This may be an issue for Buddhism in particular at the moment as images of the Buddha have been appropriated for commercial reasons.

With the use of images, you may well have to re-contextualize before you start; for example, the funny statue of a bald Chinese man was not meant to be a garden ornament but a Bodhisattva! You can have some interesting discussions with pupils about the way in which religious images are often cheapened and coarsened for commercial purposes.

Teaching war and peace can be very difficult, especially if you want to make sure that you are talking about not just past wars but contemporary conflicts. Here are the addresses of a few organizations that are very interested in war and its aftermath:

Christian CND, Mordechai Vanunu House,
162 Holloway Road, London N7 8DQ.
www.ccnd.gn.apc.org
A Church of England group committed to pacifism:
www.anglican.peacemaker.org.uk
www.baptist-peace.org.uk
Campaign Against the Arms Trade (Christian
Network): www.caat.org.uk/getinvolved/Christian
The leading Roman Catholic peace organization:
www.paxchristi.org.uk.

These organization often have excellent websites and in the case of Christian CND have produced some thoughtful material on peace issues.

If you want to get an international Christian point of view, Sojourners (a US Evangelical peace and justice movement) send out weekly email. Contact them at www.sojo.net.

One way to engage deeply with war and peace is from the website www.lewrockwell.com, which has an article about Father George Zabelka. Zabelka blessed air crews involved in the atomic bombing of Nagasaki, and came to see that nuclear war was immoral. He travelled to Japan to apologize in person for his role in the bombing and devoted his life to the nuclear protest movement.

There are many excellent organizations that will help with ideas on the teaching of world development and poverty issues. Here are some of their contact details:

**CHRISTIAN ORGANIZATIONS**

Christian Aid may be able to supply you with a local speaker, as they have been developing a network of ex-teachers to take their work into schools. Contact: Christian Aid, PO Box 100, London SE1 7RT. www.christianaid.org.
Tear Fund, 100 Church Road, Teddington TW11 8QE. www.tearfund.org.
CAFOD, Romero Close, London SW9 9TY. www.cafod.org.

**OTHER FAITHS**

One of the main Muslim development charities: www.islamic-relief.com.
A Jewish organization: Tzedek, c/o 61 Llanvanor Road, London NW2 2AR. www.tzedek.org.uk.
www.hinduaid.org.
www.unitedsikhs.org.
A Buddhist development charity: The Karuna Trust, 72 Holloway Road, London N7 8JG.
www.karunatrust.org.

**IMPORTANT NON-RELIGIOUS ORGANIZATIONS**

Oxfam, at www.oxfam.org.uk, is one of the most established development charities, founded by Quakers but now run on a non-religious basis.
The Department of International Development, at www.dfid.gov.uk, is an excellent source of information on many problems. DFID produces booklets on development themes as well as a magazine called *Developments*. They also regularly have an information centre at the Greenbelt Festival (see Idea 86).

The challenge is not to find the material in this field but to choose the very best and that which above all can make connections with pupils.

Animal rights has become a staple part of GCSE RE courses, especially the short course. There are many interrelated issues which need to be addressed. Here are some websites to help you:

> For groups protesting against ill-treatment of animals: www.rspca.org.uk is the site of the RSPCA, which has an extensive number of materials for teaching animal welfare. Also useful are the Friends of the Earth at www.foe.co.uk and Greenpeace at www.greenpeace. org.uk. There are many other groups, but be cautious about the ones that you indicate for pupils. The International Fund for Animal Welfare can be contacted at IFAW, Freepost SEA 13616, Rochester ME1 1BR.
> Vegetarian websites: www.in-site.co.uk is an excellent site, as it lists the Top 50 vegetarian sites.
> Religious sites looking at animal issues: there is an overlap with general environmental sites (see Idea 14). Yet there are others worth seeking out, including A Rocha, an international conservation charity with a Christian basis, which can be contacted on http://en.arocha.org.

Pupils are often full of opinions on these issues, but they often lack balance. Try to select material which will enable them to develop a full understanding of the material and not let them slip into cliché or one-sidedness. You will need to be very careful with the material you select in this area.

ANIMAL RIGHTS ISSUES

# A final word

## WHY DO WE HAVE TO DO RE?

Hopefully, the ideas that have been presented in the book will enable you to connect with pupils. Remember that all good RE teaching will consist of the two strands that the 1990s model syllabuses suggested: learning about and learning from strands.

Learning about is making sure that pupils know and understand the facts and the information of religion. Do they know and understand the 5 pillars of Islam?

Learning from is making sure that pupils use the religious material in order to reflect on their own experience. So they need to go beyond knowing what the 5 pillars are, to understanding the nature of discipline, belief, charity and ideas about God that are contained within, being able to give their own responses, whether religious or non-religious.

You might like to reflect on these words from Graham Swift's novel, *Waterland* (Picador, 1999). They could serve as a creed for any teacher, but especially one of RE:

*Children be curious. Nothing is worse than when curiosity stops. Nothing is more repressive than the repression of curiosity. Curiosity begets love. It weds us to this world. It is part of our perverse, madcap love for the impossible world we inhabit. People die when curiosity dies. People have to find out, people have to know. How can there be any true understanding until we know what we're made of?*